Praise for From First L

"*From First Breath to Last: A Su~~~~ ~~~~ ~~~~, womanhood, and Aging* is an honest and engaging portrayal of a topic challenging to us all. Montgomery shares intimate details in her stories that bring the reader into the room. Readers of all ages can relate to the realistic depictions included in this book, with stories that empower and inspire. This tells the tale of leadership and learning from the history of those closest to the author through the wisdom of their lived experiences. An illuminating read." — Dr. Latrissa Lee Neiworth, Ed.D., Organizational Leadership, MA Ed., IDI QA Professor of Leadership

"Dede Montgomery honors the forested paths women wander along on their life journey starting in girlhood until they leave their bodies through the tender writings of a mother and daughter through a unique lens. Gifted with her mother's, Patty Marilyn Daum Montgomery, own unpublished memoir, plus her doctoral thesis and other writings, Dede Montgomery entwines their separate journeys into a story filled with insight, reconciliation, whimsy, wisdom, and grief. I was left for a longing to have sat down and had a long chat with 'Patty,' a keenly wise and intelligent woman, who was laying the groundwork for the current movement for understanding the value of post-menopausal women in our society in her writing and as a professor-mentor to women. Dede Montgomery's own growth from childhood through young adulthood through to her caring for her mother at the end of her life reflects how, like the landscape of a forest, slowly changes over time, parental-child relationships too mature with age. Nature is a woven theme throughout *From First Breath to Last* and as you approach the end you sense Patty, like the nurse logs in a forest, is still nurturing her family, deeply loved." — Chaplain Anne Richardson, Spiritual Companion, Founder, Nurture Your Journey offering grief and loss support

"Lyrical and lovely, this readable work offers profound, poignant observations and insights on nearly every page. It deftly weaves the narrative of a daughter entering her 'crone years' with the actual diary of a fascinating mother who led an extraordinary life. It will appeal, especially, to women in midlife and beyond, who, like me, are examining, in their 'bonus years,' their own lives and relationships and choices. Ultimately, while acknowledging the complications and messiness of life, it is affirming, illuminating, and even joyful. Any mother would be thrilled by such a tender, insightful tribute from her daughter." — Mary Hoskins, retired occupational safety and health consultant and public sector executive manager

Other books by Dede Montgomery

My Music Man
Beyond the Ripples
Then, Now, and In-Between
Humanity's Grace

From
First Breath to Last

DEDE MONTGOMERY

From First Breath to Last

A STORY ABOUT LOVE, WOMANHOOD, AND AGING

GusGus Press • Bedazzled Ink Publishing
Fairfield, California

978-1-960373-40-3 paperback

Cover Design
by

Sapling
Studio

"Mourning in Pandemic Times" first published in *Plague 2020: A World
Anthology of Poetry and Art About* COVID-19 (July 2020)

GusGus Press
a division of
Bedazzled Ink Publishing Company
Fairfield, California
http://www.bedazzledink.com

Contents

To Patty, her loves and passions.

"The great thing about getting older is that you don't lose all the other ages you've been."—*Madeleine L'engle*

Place of Thanks

Smells and images: exhilarating, filling, haunting.

Before, After and Now.

Snippets of memories. What happened? What didn't? Who is to say?

Then. Buckets of sand, gulls cawing, shrieking wind and penetrating rain, sink deep into cold, wet sand. Salty tide pools warmed by fading sun. Sand pushes through cracks between my toes, into my nails. I extract my toes from the sand and run to cold, crashing waves leaving icy shivers.

Rare rays that heat and surprise.

A sky awakens with wispy pinks, preparing our hearts for incoming rain.

Stunted Pine trees hide creatures and forts of the past. Nature's imperfect perfection.

Future.

Giggles. Laughs. Shouts. Cries. Powder fresh soft elbows and knees. Creaking joints and silences. Absences.

Family and place.

Then. Fingers reach into Dixie cups, gritty ash rubbed between thumbs and forefingers. No longer. Simple gifts, tosses into welcoming dunes. Beyond tears. Going back. Gone forever.

Staring into colors fading and bursting, the impending darkness of a sunset. The end for now. Nothing else to imagine but the beauty of now.

Tomorrow there may be more buckets and sand between the toes. More sunsets. More ashes. Or not.

Of Place.

About This Book

LAST NIGHT I dreamt about my mom. I knew she wasn't going to be around much longer. She told me she wanted to write one more book; her expression invited my approval. *"Yes,"* I said. "I'd love to help you, Mom." And here we are.

Two years before Mom died, I suggested we write a book together. We would share our mother-daughter, aging together journey; I would write while she offered insights. Soon after I posted a few blogs. When asked, she confirmed her trust in me to write about her.

While Patty lived her last four months in our home, I outlined and prewrote the book, less sure as the days passed that I would complete it. The subject felt tired and overwritten: what could I say about our mother-daughter expedition that hadn't yet been said by others? Mom died, and I left those early musings alone for seven months. Recently I began wondering if it might be a future project, yet felt unsure. Until last night's dream.

I recently read *Peony in Love* by Lisa See. As I neared its final pages, I was struck by the synchronicity between its plot with my attempt to make sense of the story I wanted to tell about Mom. Yes, I slowly understood. While See weaves stories shared by deceased ancestor wives, why not invite my own mother, who died in 2021, to inform this book?

My mother was my childhood caregiver, best friend, and later, the loved one I cared for in her final days. Patty was of the "silent generation" growing up during the depression. She struggled with low self-esteem and sometimes felt weighed down by expectation, even though she was top in each of her classes and excelled in most everything she took on. She completed bachelor, master, and doctorate degrees and raised me, her only daughter of five children, to be self-confident and self-assured. She followed in what she believed was the expected path for other women like her who were privileged by whiteness, education, and middle-class income. Until she couldn't.

She broke loose with support from some and criticism by others. She lived a long, full, and satisfying life, but died occasionally needing to be reminded about the gifts she gave others during her life and those she would leave behind.

From First Breath to Last is a mosaic of memories, events, and reflections about Patty Montgomery, our relationship, and insights into the generations and circumstances we were born into that informed the women we became. Patty was unique among her contemporaries. I was born thirty years later and faced expectations and barriers different to both her generation and that of my own daughters born three decades later.

This book is influenced by hundreds of pages of Patty's unpublished memoir: her hopes, dreams, wishes, and lessons. Included are Patty's words directly excerpted from her memoir; a chapter from her 1994 book (*Mythmaking: Heal Your Path, Claim Your Future*) and sections of her 1986 doctorate dissertation (*The Experience of a Critical Event Leading to Dramatic Midlife Career Change for Women.*) My words augment hers to illustrate the intersection of our lives. I tried to be honest, authentic, and sensitive as I wrote and weaved her selected writing together as if Mom was at my side. I will look to my dreams to know how well I did.

The Things I Know Now

IT MADE NO sense to me when I first learned Mom ate sugar sandwiches as a child. Once I tried to replicate that dry barely sweet snack to see how it tasted, but I knew to be authentic I had to use white bread with the tiniest bit of butter to hold it and the white sugar together. I grew up delighting in an occasional breakfast treat of cinnamon and sugar toast, but the sugar sandwich tasted awful. I didn't understand how this hardly fit to be called a sandwich could be considered anything desired. It wasn't until later I understood the sandwiches to be a treat of the time; and also a concrete reminder of all Mom and her sisters mostly didn't get back in those times.

Mom was of the generation growing up during the Great Depression and World War II. Newly married nearly two decades later, Mom joined other middle and upper class young American women whose main focus was to raise children, even as others protested Vietnam and argued for racial and sexual equity. If asked, I'm certain Mom would tell others she was not racially prejudiced: after all, one of her best male high school friends was Black, she encouraged a play date between me and one of the few Black boys in our rural community, and a decade later she taught Head Start with mostly Hispanic children whose parents were migrant agricultural workers. Yet, she dismissed my question when I asked if she would have ever dated the young high school friend, something she could not have imagined during those late 1940s.

Peers in my generation were too young to serve in Vietnam, and my friends and I instead protested on Mothers Days at Montana's Maelstrom Airforce Base. We worried about nuclear winter and the cold war, and environmental catastrophes like Love Canal. Like some of my white-privileged peers, I believed things were getting better for all people; unknowingly selecting my trusted sources to tell me equity was *en route*. A decade later, some of us rocked babies to news of the war in Iraq, and not long after were teary and wordless as we tried to explain 9-11 to our elementary-aged kids.

Now those daughters of mine are grown adults, who anxiously shoulder the burdens of climate change devastation, uncontrolled gun violence, and untrustworthy politicians. They believe their generation will never be able to afford what their grandparents claimed as the American Dream, and some of them question if it is even their dream. This would make Mom sad if she were with us still today: she loved her grandchildren as much as life itself.

Among my most treasured childhood summer memories are the "midnight" walks Mom invented, inviting me and my two younger brothers to tag along. The still darkness was frightfully thrilling, though our brains promised safety as we walked along our rural lane. Leftover warmth from the daytime's sun tickled our bare arms and legs; ripening blackberries created the aroma of Willamette River Summer. As we spotted car headlights in the distance we would scamper to a hiding place safe from the shine of car lights; our hearts pounded as we crouched into the darkness to remain hidden from the driver. Those years we kids sometimes played a game our older cousins called "German Spotlight," a pastime others called flashlight tag. German Spotlight was never as exciting as the midnight walks when we hid from cars. It was only after Mom died that I read details in her memoir about the nightmares caused during World War II and stories of Hitler and Nazis. Although I had read much of her memoir aloud to her in her final years, I had never chosen to read that section. I wonder now if her children's reference of German Spotlight ever troubled her, or it was simply accepted like so many other things.

It seems I always knew the joyful memories Mom retained from the Victory Garden her father planted on their extra Northeast Portland lot. Mom shared other stories with me about how, as a girl, she would bus to her summer job somewhere out in East County to string green beans. Although my brothers and I also grew up with a large garden, mostly created by our mom, and we even picked strawberries for cash in the summer, it took me awhile to understand her green bean job that consisted only of putting up string. Back then I imagined her sitting down with a bucket of green beans on a table and tying string around each bean pod rather than securing strings and supports for pole beans to latch on by climbing vines.

I don't know when I first learned that some people and times expected women to be virgins before they got married even though men seemed to be excluded from this rule. I knew some girls in my high school class were having sex, and they most certainly were not married. For a girl like me in family with four brothers, this double standard made me angry: the older I got, the more gender inequities I uncovered. Even though I had already seen signs of gender bias, I didn't know then what to call it other than to refer to people who talked like that as male chauvinist pigs, a description popular in those 1970s.

Being born in 1933, Mom was part of what some call the Silent Generation. She pushed back against many gendered expectations, especially during mid-life and celebrated what felt to her like new opportunities created for women born into newer generations like mine. By being born in 1961, I am the youngest of the Boomers, yet I too pushed back against gender expectations for girls of my time. I played boys Little League baseball when invited by a coach who was a friend of my brother's, and I was enraged when I learned my Portland cousins could wear pants to school but those of us in rural Wilsonville were not allowed. When I got to junior high, I asked the school administrators, then living in more conservative Eastern Oregon, why I had to take home economics when all the boys were assigned shop class.

My two daughters and their female cousins are Millennials. They have had access to nearly as many opportunities as boys and have found the same traps around athletic competition. Yet, they too were in their late teens and twenties when #MeToo took hold, and we all were devastated to be reminded things hadn't changed as fast or as much as we had hoped or may have naively believed.

The older Mom got, the more I understood the impact of the shame she carried from childhood and enduring into early womanhood. Patty toiled through the work—writing, learning, counseling, spiritual seeking to process and move through both guilt and shame. I believe she died at peace, to the degree that any of us can when we go without food and water in our final days. But because of the dementia she experienced late in life, I'll never know if it was complete. Toward the end of her life I acknowledged and thanked her for helping me learn the importance of addressing our own personal demons before we hit old age: before failing bodies, minds, or spirits prevent us from doing so. But now I wonder if that belief is naïve. Maybe what's true is we can heal only so much in a single lifetime on earth. Might there be trauma that runs too deep, creating scars however faint they may look to others, that linger on until we take our last breath? We do the best we can to process, accept and move on. And if we were to time travel back to the late 1970s, Mom would tell me—this is why we reincarnate.

I remember when Mom first told me about the guilt she took on as a twelve-year-old after her family suffered a significant tragedy. Her toddler nephew, who was visiting their Northeast Portland childhood home, died after accidentally pushing through the screen in an upstairs window. Patty wrote about this experience in her memoir, and decades after it happened, addressed it repeatedly with a therapist and her sister, the parent of her nephew. During my own early motherhood, I remember when a neighbor's child died this way, and how the family moved out of the home and neighborhood not long after. The older I get, the more I understand how this loved one's death created deep guilt and shame for Mom, even though others didn't blame her. And although she found closure forty-one years later with her sister, I'm beginning to understand how closure doesn't heal all lasting wounds.

Mom also wrote and later talked openly about another deeply personal and significant cause of shame in her life. She worked diligently for decades beginning at early mid-life to understand and accept the details of the events, learn not to blame herself, and to confront and forgive the person who caused the pain. I am grateful she felt safe to share these most difficult and impactful lifetime markers with me and others she was close to and trusted. These are powerful life experiences woven into the mosaic of who she was.

Patty loved being a mother and grandmother. She demonstrated it with each of her children, and all of her grandchildren. Since her death, two great-grandchildren have been born, including one from my daughter. It's hard not to feel renewed loss in my inability to share that with her and Dad now. She had an innate gift to know how to make each one of us feel special, and even when she had her own stressors she recovered to the degree of catching up where she left off.

> I needn't have worried about how to be a grandmother— it came naturally. I fell in love all over again as each was born, just as I had with my own children. My heart filled to overflowing. My teaching actually became a distraction and disruption for me as I created as much time with them as possible.

This helps me understand that we aren't necessarily programmed to be the way our parents were: her mother was a kind, albeit removed, grandmother to me, my brothers, and cousins, but she was nothing close to the grandmother Patty was.

When Mom broke her hip at eighty-four years of age, my first thoughts and fears were informed by my remembrances of her own mother. Our Grandma Daum broke a hip in her early seventies, after which she lost interest in food and began to lose weight. Never holding a driver's license, she had relied throughout her adult life on buses, streetcars, and walking to get to her connections at church and playing piano in meal centers. She died not long after the hip fracture, living alone in an apartment with ample visits from Mom and less often, her other daughters. When Mom broke her hip at eighty-four, I knew the data; few elderly walk again after suffering broken hips and many die within the year. Mom walked again—that determination she demonstrated throughout her life recognizable yet with the shadow of exhaustion and dementia. I led her through her prescribed physical therapy routine, reminding her "no pain, no gain" and "you snooze you lose": phrases she would smile but roll her eyes at. Once with a bit of a laugh she told me to shut up. She did live nearly four more years and walked again, though more slowly, but the traumatic rehab experience aged her.

Mom shared how much her mother embarrassed her when she was a teenager, but later regretted how mean she felt she and her five sisters had been to her during those years. Patty loved her mother and yet it was her oldest sisters who mothered her: sewed her clothes and modeled motherhood when they had children. Both Mom's parents, my grandparents, lost their own mothers when young and were brought up by older siblings: oh, how much we are molded because of what happens to our parents and the trauma they too experience. My grandmother sang in church choirs, played piano often when she visited us and extended that love of music to "men in the soup kitchens." But she couldn't keep house or keep up with the duties many of us expect from a parent. Mom and her sisters learned to do all that, embarrassed if visitors dropped by when the house was a mess. It was only later as Mom and two of her sisters experienced advancing macular degeneration that she wondered if the food spots and other signs of uncleanliness later in her mother's life, something Mom once attributed to her inability to care for herself, might have resulted from impaired vision that she never spoke about.

Our mom played the leading role in taking care of her mother to the end of her life. I was then a Lincoln High student, full on determined to get top grades and be the best athlete I could be. I was small and scrappy and worked hard to be as good as a few girls who had more natural talent and size than me. Mom was on track to being burned out working full time in special education after receiving her masters at Portland State University and married to a man who had not accepted his need for recovery. Yet, with all that, of the six daughters, she was the dominant caregiver for her mother. Patty's youngest sister recently told me that it was Patty who always seemed to care about others. To that I am certain her friends would shout Amen!

Mom told me she didn't want me to be "stuck" taking care of her at the end of her life. Yet, when it happened, it wasn't like that. Unlike what I've seen with parents of some of my friends, she tried to prevent me from needing to do that. When Dad died she moved into Assisted Living, a facility she had already selected with my help that was walking distance to both her last apartment and my home. I once told her I would invite her to live with us, but the stairs in our home would be unsafe, and she would be isolated as I left for work each day in those days before my work became remote during the pandemic.

She insisted she didn't want that, neither to be a burden but also for her own independence.

That independence she kept—until she couldn't. I was there every step of the way. Maybe it's because we saw ourselves as best friends. I've read since her death that daughters shouldn't look at their mothers as best friends. I disagree. Maybe it was because she had been the mother that her kids and all our friends felt comfortable sharing most anything with. Maybe it is because I'm the only daughter of five children and for the last thirty-one years lived in closest proximity to her and Dad. Maybe it's because mostly Mom and I "got" each other, a feeling that only deepened as I too became a mother.

That's not to say we hadn't had difficult times. Mom was there for me when I made my decision, summer before college, to schedule an appointment with Planned Parenthood to be fitted with a diaphragm. Although I was among those high school girls who remained a virgin, I knew I didn't want to be one in college. She waited in the passenger seat of the car while I had my appointment and then took me to lunch. Only two years later, though, she taught me how uncomfortable it was to have your mom talk to you about sex as if she was a young teenager again. Even though Mom and Dad were newly divorced then and none of us suspected they'd remarry later, I wanted to support her. But it was too weird. What did she think, I wondered then? That we could talk "friend to friend" about things like that, when I wasn't that comfortable talking about sex yet? It was a decade later when I understood. So many women of Mom's generation were raised without freedom to experiment or even discuss their sexuality: how exciting and freeing it must have been for her to experience this, even if she was in her late forties. She was able to find then and for the first time, some of the independence that many of us born in the 1960s expected.

Mom apologized years later about sharing with me those first days of experimenting with sex outside of marriage. It was a heady time for her to feel free with her sexuality, and it had seemed only natural to want to share it with her close college-aged daughter. She later understood how odd that was for me. Later, she also explained about a time when I was thirteen and we were at a family summer camp, where she was a counselor for those a bit older than me. We were playing a game of volleyball with the two of us on the same team. She acted oddly competitive toward me, something foreign as she had only always been supportive of my athleticism. These years later, she told me how she suddenly had felt angry and excited all mixed up together, seeing me as young and beautiful with all these years and opportunities ahead of me in these freer days of the 1970s. Ripe with opportunities she had never experienced at my age.

Our mom made tremendous differences in the lives of many people, especially women, through her friendships and as a teacher and mentor. I know she was proud to be an author, but even beyond the accomplishment of publishing, she was focused on the possibility that her book might make a difference in the lives of women. Attendees to the workshops and courses she taught, especially those held at Marylhurst University, remarked on the power she created in her connections. I attended one, my three-year-old daughter on my lap and was impressed. I wish now I had a recording of it. And Mom knew it too.

> Within every class there was a palpable feeling of connection, acceptance and questioning of old cultural values. I often felt, particularly after my "Mothers and Daughters" class, that there was a "presence" in the room. I understood it scientifically as a morphic field that occurs when a group of conscious people are together over a period of time, such a field develops around them. There is a sense of sacredness in such groups, and it was palpable for most of us. I realized that I didn't have to teach classes on spirituality, but simply live as if every moment and every person mattered.

As I read this today, I recognize the parts of Mom that I inherited: I too feel I create a sense of connection with groups I speak to or with. Even as much as I knew about and shared most everything with Mom, it sometimes overwhelms me now to discover topics in a different light that I wish we could talk about.

I know now how overwhelming it feels when a loved one enters hospice. The day Mom was accepted into hospice, living with us now in the heart of the pandemic and sleeping in my family's dining room, I received morphine and drugs we may need to keep her comfortable.

Five weeks later I sat with Mom, she having not moved out of her hospital bed since that hospice acceptance, for the five days between her last food and drink and her last breath. During her final weeks, I read to her from her memoir, together with other favorite books. We listened to special music from her life: Broadway show tunes, favored CDs from classical composers and New Age musicians. I told her how much I loved her, joined by other beloved family members. She was visited by her children, grandchildren, sisters, a niece, and a few friends.

When I was young I thought I wanted to live forever and I wanted my parents to do that too. Life experience has proven this so wrong. Now, at sixty-two with my own mortality closer than it had been after previous birthdays, I'm slowly getting it. Yes, I want to live forever because I want to know my daughters and my grandkids, I want to walk in the forests and paddle in the rivers. I want to know that wars end and that our climate change reverses course. I still want that but every day, I get closer to the truth. Then none of us ever fully know. Let me be ready and to have appreciated all that I've received, even the parts that felt unfair or crappy. Make sure I have told those around me the love I have for them while we're still here.

Now I know what it feels like to be with the two people you have loved your entire life—who brought you into this world—take their last breaths: Dad's simply slowing and dwindling, Mom's as last rattled gasps. I know what it is to feel sorrow and relief simultaneously. To flash back to a scene of having them placed into the bag which will be their last cozy spot before becoming ashes and dust. I hope I can always recall the feeling of those ashes, and small remnants of bones sift through my hand into the current of the Willamette River that they both loved so much, into the ocean, and in the great spaces above a favorite hiking trail.

All these things I know now: some I understand, others I find hard to accept. My mom's own writings, some shared here, help me tease out where some of them came from and the lessons that exist for those of us moving through life later.

What Makes Us?
From Patty's unpublished memoir, 2008

I FELT VERY secure until I was five years old, oblivious to the uncertainties of my family life. I was the only one of my sisters who had Mother to herself for such a long period of time. I felt loved, attended to, and special when she took me for long walks through the neighborhood. She, like I, always noticed children playing as well, stopping to talk to them (which embarrassed me at the time, though I do it, too). She especially loved looking at peoples' yards and gardens.

Perhaps being the fifth of six daughters, as well as having an intuitive sense that all was not as it seemed, gave me an unnatural urge for the excitement and chaos of change. Many of the things that happened in my life, particularly my history of auto-immune disorders, may be the result of my "high" when I was running on adrenaline. At any rate, I think that as a result of all of that, I was shaped into an obedient, helpful, cooperative chameleon-like child who intuited another's emotions and responded accordingly. I saw both sides of all arguments and had a hard time making a decision until all the evidence was in—which never happened.

Because I perceived I was not always safe, I seemed to have an antenna that was constantly on the lookout for emotional tension and undercurrents, and I sought ways to avoid or remedy them. I either withdrew in self-protection or tried to take care of the other person—usually my mother. It was the breeding ground for the perfect co-dependent personality. I became mother's ally when I was old enough to notice how badly my sisters treated her, even though I had conflicted feelings by then. The downside of this quality was that I took on other's pain and burdens at my own expense. I believed it was up to me to solve others' problems. If I couldn't do that, I was a failure.

And yet, dear Mom—perhaps at your expense—this quality made you into a perfect listener and confidante for your children and friends. I know you weren't always successful as you tried to seek a balance later in life to protect your own boundaries yet still be fully available for others.

Though the dark side of our "perfect family" was the shabbiness and untidiness of our home, we were forced by economic circumstances to become independent at an early age. Our family was an anomaly in our lower-middle class neighborhood during the Depression because of my parents dedication to music and the value of education. Being college graduates, they made it clear we would all go to college, always holding us to very high academic standards. Dad's father was a teacher, principal, then superintendent of a Kansas school district who deeply valued books and learning above all else. We owned a set of encyclopedias and a few of the classics, but most of our books came from the school and neighborhood library.

You gifted us the love of libraries and books—weaving literacy into the lives of your children and grandchildren. Immediately after you died, it was impossible for me to go to our local library without remembering the times we walked its floors together, searching out books, relishing its unique smells and whispered voices. Those are dear memories for me now.

Our school librarian introduced us to most of the children's classic books and held annual "Treasure Island" contests, challenging each of us to read as many books as we could. I remember the pride of winning the competitions often, bringing home a blue or silver ribbon, along with a book of my very own. She and our music teacher, spinsters like most elementary school teachers then, loved and lived what they taught, and left deep impressions on me. Perhaps it was genetic as well, but those teachers and my beloved second grade teacher laid the foundation for my own teaching ambition. In my third year of college at Monmouth, then a teacher's college, my favorite class was Children's Literature, in which we were introduced to the finest in children's literature—books that had been published since I was eleven, winning Caldecott and other book awards. I actually made a card file of each book that I read, later buying or bringing those books home from the library to read to my children and, later, my grandchildren.

I sigh. We too read Caldecott award winners and other children book favorites in your last years of life when I was reading to you! You laughed and cried at *Charlotte's Web, Make Way for Ducklings* and *Blueberries for Sal*. We twice read cover to cover about the journeys of Mr. Toad, Badger, and Mole in *Wind in the Willows*. Books brought such joy to both of us during my childhood and in your final years. I await the moments when I too will share these treasures with my grandchildren, your great grands; one of many lasting gifts.

Our father gifted us the love of Shakespeare. He took the four of us to Medford every summer when he was visiting an insurance client. We camped out at various campsites along the Rogue River, and thus started a family tradition of attending Shakespeare plays in Ashland. The exposure to such fine theater left a mark on all of us, and we carried it into our married lives for many years and the next generations.

Music was always in the foreground of our family life. Mother loved to sing, at home and in church choirs. I have many happy memories of her playing the piano for us while we danced or marched around and around the edge of the big living room rug. I'm sure that she was happiest when she was singing, lost in another world far away from family concerns. Her repertoire varied, as she could play almost anything by ear, effortlessly combining chords and verse— Mendelssohn's "Songs Without Words," religious music, Stephen Foster, popular songs.

I was sad, Mom, that you weren't also comfortable playing by ear. I remember trying to encourage you to sit and play piano in your final years; you felt without good enough vision to read music, you would be disappointed to not play well. I take this as a lesson.

Just before she died in 1978, a tea was held in my mother's honor for her thirty years of singing in church choirs. It meant a great deal to her, and it was then I realized Mother was perceived by others in a way far different from those of her critical daughters. During my high school years, Mother began playing the piano at the Salvation Army chapel's evening services in Old Town. I was embarrassed that she would do such a thing and was relieved that she never brought "those people" home for dinner. While we were all critical of her for that type of community service, I know that her gentle spirit and depth of religious beliefs quieted and soothed many a restless soul living on the streets.

In your final months when our conversations lagged, we listened to classical music during the day and different musicals each evening for dinner hour as you sat propped up in your hospital bed. You smiled and even sang along with Mary Martin in *South Pacific,* and other leading men and women in original soundtracks of *Oklahoma, Carousel,* and *Sound of Music.*

I now realize that, in many ways, our family repeated the pattern of a single-parent household. We were "motherless" daughters with a mother lacking mature, responsible, and dependable parental behavior. Without a role model as woman and wife, we had to make our own way with help from each other. As a result, I was profoundly shaped by my oldest sisters, learning from them how to be a girl, and then a young woman—and, later how to be a mother and a grandmother.

During those impressionable early years, coincidental with many happy and warm times as an earnest, budding Christian, several things happened that caused me great shame and stress over my conflicting feelings about Mother. I was ashamed of Mother because she couldn't manage a household like other mothers. At church, I became even more aware of the difference when, at five, I was chosen to be in a Christmas play. Some of the mothers were fitting us in costumes, and as I took off my dress, I heard a mother "tsk tsk" and say to another woman: "Look at Patty's dirty underwear! What's wrong with her mother?" My face burned as shame flooded over me. "How could I be responsible for my mother's negligence?" I wondered, internalizing the shame.

I adored my Aunt Emily, Memmie, the eldest of seven children, who was the caregiver for Mother and her siblings at thirteen when their mother died. For several summers, I took the bus to Spokane to spend a week or so alone with Memmie. I felt completely loved and safe in her humble, clean, orderly home with strict limits and high expectations that were tempered with love and affection. However, I have one vivid memory of a time when I corrected a word or a phrase that one of the neighbor children said. Memmie called me aside and scolded me for acting "smarty," and I was left with a sense of embarrassment and shame for standing out from the crowd. It was probably the beginning of my unease and tendency to blush.

Memories wash over me—of our chaotic laundry room, dirty and clean clothes piled up, un-ironed clothes stashed in disarray, with barely an aisle to find one's way to the back. When I was eight, and we finally had an electric washing machine and automatic wringer, I accidentally got my hand in the wringer. I was taken to the doctor, had my fingernail removed, and then was scolded by mother for being careless. We also hung our clothes on lines in the basement or backyard. As my sisters and I took on housekeeping chores, we merely stuffed everything into the drawers as quickly as possible. For years I've had dreams of that laundry room, the dark basement with lines full of clothes needing to be folded, and of messy closets, drawers, and cupboards. I am still uneasy with disorder and confusion. I was sent home from school once, for having lice in my hair, and another time for an uncontrollable nosebleed, which troubled me throughout my childhood. I remember "weighing day": taking my shoes off in the gym, waiting to be weighed, and kids teasing me about the holes in my socks. Another experience of shame came from the comments by the head librarian. A combination of carelessness on my part, and the disorder in our home, I continually returned books late, losing several. She scolded me quite severely, giving me a lecture on responsibility. That was one of two that deeply affected me, the second occurring during high school.

The ultimate result of all of those shame-based memories, and others that surfaced later was my confusion over being female because of conflicting feelings about my mother. Upset by the verbal aggressiveness and lack of respect shown toward mother by my father and sisters, I took a sympathetic approach, defending and trying to protect her. I remember going off to school at about seven, and running back to kiss Mother goodbye, as I believed something terrible might happen to her if I failed to do so. It is called "magical thinking," and I saw later that it was a defensive reaction to the fear, believing that my morning kiss could protect her from bad things.

And, Mom, I wish I could tell you again: you provided for your own children a safe, loving, and protective home. Yes, later at your own expense. And you taught me that each of us can do better than our parents; genetics doesn't dictate all.

The world changed on Sunday morning, December 7, 1941, when I was eight. I remember hearing Dad, agitated as he listened to the radio, and then yelling about the bombing of Pearl Harbor. In the morning, I saw the bold, threatening headline in the newspaper as he read it with shaking hands. I barely understood the concept of war, though I knew peripherally Dad had fought in France during "The Great War." I think the fact that my father was in WW I and never talked about it created a worse horror of war than had he talked about his experiences. I thought he was a "cook" in the war, not knowing the battles and loss of army mates that he suffered through. World War II became a greater and immediate terror. We were fortunate that no one within our family was injured or killed during the war.

In 1942, Dad and my sister Dorothy, at seventeen, went to work in the shipyards as welders. They left early in the morning, Dorothy looking gorgeous, with bright red lipstick, blonde hair in a forties pompadour, wearing men's pants and shirt, boots, with hardhat and metal lunchbox. She began as a welder but was recognized quickly as being very smart and was trained as an electrician. She looked so beautiful and patriotic. I was very proud of her for daring to go out into a man's world, and bragged to my friends that she was in the shipyards working "for the war effort." That was my first taste of feminism, when women ventured into a "man's world."

People were urged to conserve materials that were strategic in the war effort, going to the extreme of saving bacon fat which reportedly contained a chemical used to make gunpowder. Voluntary conservation was not adequate, however, and in 1942 the government rationed meat, butter, sugar, gas, tires, even shoes (two pairs a year for civilians). As a nine-year-old, I was dismayed that my favorite penny candies, chocolate candy bars, and marshmallows were unavailable. There was a huge political discussion after so many complaints about the butter substitute, "oleo", an unappealing white solid spread. To make it more palatable, Marjorie, the wife of Oregon's liberal Senator Neuberger, fought for a law to allow food coloring to be used. From then on, a small tube of yellow food dye came with the box of oleo.

Because of an imminent possibility of Japanese submarines bombing Oregon, there were blackouts every evening. My father volunteered to be block warden. He went out every evening, wearing a hard hat, carrying a flashlight, checking to be sure shades were down in the houses in our block. Many families had gold and silver stars in their windows, showing the world their loss.

There was no way to escape the war. Part of my mental terror was the propaganda: newspapers, radios, and movies screamed of battles, terrifying posters pasted around the city caricaturizing "the Japs" as apes, the Nazis with evil faces. Our greatest shame as a culture was seizing all the properties of anyone of Japanese descent and putting them into internment camps. Since there were few Japanese in my neighborhood, I lost no friends personally, but was aware that our country had a deep, dark secret. That was the beginning of my nightmares: recurring dreams about Nazis taking over our town, storming through the streets with weapons and ugly, fearful voices and strides; images from the movies putting me in frigid Norway during the German occupation trying to get away from the monsters of war; running, running, being chased and unable to run fast enough, someone following me, fear enshrouding me. Over and over. The nightmares were reinforced by the Newsreels at the movie theaters, blaring out war news and horrific photos. Love was romanticized, but even the forties movies had an edge to the stories and songs, such as "Someone to Watch Over Me," that haunted me later with feelings of sadness, courage, pain, loss, and dying.

We younger girls had wartime responsibilities as well and caught the patriotic fever. At school we learned to crochet scarves for the soldiers and wrap gauze bandages for the Red Cross. We assisted Dad with his huge "Victory Garden"—an empty adjacent lot that Dad had wisely purchased when he bought the 1920s home in 1942 for $3500. I was active in a 4-H Club for several years, receiving a badge for helping with Dad's Victory Garden. All the Portland grade schools sponsored events and contests for the war effort. There were newspaper and tin can drives, as aluminum was scarce. Everyone was expected to wash and flatten cans, so we children went around with wagons to collect them from households in our neighborhood. I was extremely ambitious and competitive, and received a blue ribbon and named "Queen in Tincania" in the sixth grade (1944). We also collected newspapers, tying them with string, and took them by wagon to a collection area. I received a second prize, then a Grand Prize ribbon for the paper drive in the sixth grade.

Queen in Tincania, Mom? How did I not know until after you died! Even when I thought I had paid attention to everything; I hadn't. So, instead, I smile and cry as I think of my mom, Patty Daum, as Tincania Queen.

An irony about my childhood is that from the outside, we were viewed as the "perfect" family. All of my friends loved my father, who was funny, affectionate, and generous. When I was in high school, he'd pack lunches with thick slices of meatloaf or sliced beef, add a thermos of coffee, and drive several of us up to ski on Mt. Hood. He waited patiently in the car, eating his lunch, reading the Sunday newspaper while we skied. One of my high school friends told me recently that she remembers going home and talking about me, and all of my accomplishments in high school. Finally, her mother said angrily, "I don't want to hear any more about Perfect Patty. You're just as good, smart, and as popular as she is!"

My father and mother, products of midwestern values, expected us to be dependable, conscientious, and honest. We learned well how to follow the rules and regulations. We learned to achieve and tried to excel. We were hardworking and industrious. More than anything, I wanted my father's approval.

One of their shared values, unfortunately, was an externally oriented standard of behavior, such as that implied in Mother's rhetorical question "What would the neighbors think?" This query followed anything that we did in public. Most offensive and frightening to her was what we might be doing in a parked car with a boy. She assumed the worst. It was deeply shaming for her if we sat in the car in front of the house, which we did only because of our curfew. We figured that as long as we were near the house, Dad would consider us home on time. One of my sisters became so exasperated with Mother's accusations after several years, that she said, "As long as she's accusing me of doing all those bad things, I might as well do them!" She didn't—we were good girls.

And What About Us Kids?

EVEN WHEN MOM was alive, I wondered why her five kids turned out the way we did. My four brothers and I traded notes about it: each holding versions of a related but differently shaped past. Mom had shared her life journey with us, including the excerpts in the preceding chapter, *What Makes Us*. I'm not sure any of us read her memoir in its entirety when first offered, although I read many parts to her aloud in her last several years. Today, two years after her death, I ponder my own upbringing. As I weave her story with mine, I too consider how my spouse and I raised our daughters and how they may parent their own. Others have written about the factors that influence the person we become. Our genetics, familial trauma, environmental exposures, birth order, privileges, and challenges: the list goes on and on, each element unraveling and intersecting in a unique way, augmented by new research findings.

I queried my brothers about how their childhood, our parents, and our upbringing impacted self-confidence, esteem, and achievement. The five of us acknowledge our Mom's super-achieving tendencies. We also related how Dad acknowledged being satisfied to pass through school with average grades, even though we knew him to be a gifted writer and storyteller. Although an overachiever, Mom was also an early childhood educator who intentionally asserted the importance for kids to have freedom to play and create. Our childhood was flooded with hours of unscheduled time, and we were encouraged to be independent and curious. This belief and her love of nature made her an equal partner for our parents' decision to move out of our Southwest Portland neighborhood to the rural banks of the Willamette River when I was three. I am certain my childhood backdrop is a driver to who I am today: my traits, loves, and challenges.

We joined other kids of the 1960s, free from helicopter parents and arduous extracurricular schedules. Yes, we took swim lessons and played Little League, but we were also invited to explore woods and rivers; to allow our imaginations to run wild. *My Music Man* is filled with stories set in early Wilsonville: forts, forests dotted with white and pink flowered springtime trillium; dips searching for the warmest spot in the Willamette River as ripening blackberries and fishy riverbanks created the pungent smell of river summer. Mom was engaged in community activities before returning first to teach Head Start, then working as the town's kindergarten teacher, leaving a younger brother and me to be latchkey kids a few days a week. We made double-decker peanut butter saltine sandwiches, often watching afterschool specials or cartoons on TV. And we owned those afternoons to do what we might without supervision.

We all turned out okay, even with a plethora of emergency room visits. We learned to be comfortable with and crave independence, discovery, and the out-of-doors. I remember sometimes being lonely and wishing for neighbor girlfriends, and yet I loved my childhood. I spent hours tossing the ball at my brothers' pitch-back net, arranging dolls for a school day while using carbon paper to create their homework assignments, and leading my younger brothers in play in our nearby woods. It was all pretty idyllic. Except for the traumatic events that came from our parents' relationship struggles and our dad's alcoholism.

Today, I speculate Mom's awareness of her own struggles and demons influenced the way she brought us up. Not one of us five kids ever felt either of our parents expected too much from us, and yet they celebrated the successes we found. Our parents were not the helicoptering parents of the 1990s. If I could go back and query Mom now, I would ask her if she consciously planned how to keep us from feeling as she had: driven to achieve at all costs, or if it simply happened intuitively. Mom was the one we approached to ask permission to do something. We thought it was because Dad was stricter and Mom was lenient. Nonsensically, back then I figured it all made sense as after all, Mom voted Democrat while in those days Dad supported the Republican ticket. But now I wonder? Was it Mom's way of helping her kids not play it safe? Or to help teach us not to be so driven to be perfect or feel ashamed if we weren't? I now suspect it wasn't that Dad was strict as much as fearful of his loved ones getting hurt.

Mom's voluminous memoir gifts us the ability to look back at how she felt when in the throes of early and late parenthood. Much of this section of her memoir includes excerpts from the journal she kept. In it I learn she was eager to return to teaching after marrying, then living in southwest Portland. Yet, once her first son arrived, there seemed no question she would stay home. Mom's solution was to create an in-home preschool, adding her first two sons to the mix of six other children. She adored her kids and those early years but began to pull back from neighborhood evening social events involving her middle class white neighbors, teenage babysitters easy to find. Weekly female "kaffe klatches" evolved into evening couple gatherings with dancing and alcohol and, as Mom alludes to, "playing around." She and Dad withdrew. Mom knew she didn't want to add more events with alcohol into Dad's life; it flowed freely in his work world, with alcohol an expected part of wooing advertising clients. Mom's own mother was a vocal teetotaler, and Mom barely drank: this type of society felt foreign to her.

Mom was depressed not long after suffering two miscarriages before my birth in 1961. It was the day after learning they had a sister with Mom still in the hospital that my brothers decided they would beat me up. My grandmother let them know they needed to "protect" me; which my then three year-old brother translated to "tect"—something I'm certain he thought was a type of wrestling move. Even then, I know I was welcomed into this family, maybe even more so by being a girl. The humor my siblings and I have expressed throughout our lives has bonded the five of us. Our dad, even when drinking, was the ultimate crafter of hilarious one liners, even during tough times.

Mom's memoir moves along chronologically to include joyful journal recollections as two new sons are added to our mix, along with reports of our move to rural Wilsonville. She was the one to rototill rich loamy soil and plant our garden boasting sweet peas, green beans, and cucumbers. She took advanced lifesaving while pregnant with our youngest brother, a class filled with mostly teenage boys, to assure our river safety. She too identified the stress that clouded our family. Dad's drinking and working, then in a family-owned advertising business, coupled with his own financial worries as the primary financial provider for our growing family rose prominently. Mom worried about her divorced parents, her father newly remarried to a woman only six years older than her. I did not remember that our grandfather limited contact with our family for six years, only to visit us again after my dad pleaded to him to visit. My memories of my grandfather are good ones of weekend dinners and overnight family beach trips, but they are toward the end of his life and after his second wife died by stroke.

Most powerfully, Dad's drinking initiated the unraveling of Mom's religious beliefs. When we moved from Portland, our parents transferred us from the more conservative Portland Episcopal church where most of us were baptized to a liberally minded Episcopal church in Lake Oswego. I sang in the choir, and we loved the less elaborate pomp and circumstance rituals with attention to community and social action. One of my clearest memories is of cutting a blue or pink hyacinth from our garden for Easter flowering of the cross, inhaling its spicy sweet perfume.

Patty's faith was altered in 1968 coinciding with Dad's increased drinking with us five kids ranging from three to twelve years of age. As she joined her first Al-Anon group she wrote:

> I felt I was caught in the squirrel cage of alcoholism, not knowing how to survive in an emotionally wrought relationship or how to protect my children.

It was a year later Mom met one of her closest friends and mentor, Alison, also a teacher with an alcoholic spouse. Mom had recently begun reading Eastern philosophy and felt confused by the divide between that and her traditional Christian upbringing. Alison invited Mom into an Association for Research and Enlightenment (ARE) meditation group, ARE founded by the psychic Edgar Cayce. She too introduced us kids soon after to a glorious family summer camp where we were exposed to New Thought beliefs and philosophies different than that of our traditional religious education— reincarnation, meditation, karma, and the lasting belief for me of many paths to spirituality. Dad never joined us then. I must believe he felt threatened and excluded by this new pursuit.

At the risk of jumping ahead, it is powerful to acknowledge how several years later it was Alcoholics Anonymous and its higher power beliefs that spoke to Dad, strengthened by his own Christian upbringing. Today, in retrospect, I can view the big picture of how their spirituality evolved, diverged, and united but at a different place than where they began.

Our parents' eventual reunion was rare and nearly a miracle. Three decades after these difficult years of our childhood and our parents' remarriage, our parents joined my young family at our selected spiritual home where we honored the many paths to spirituality. Although Dad remained true to his traditional Christian beliefs, he adored the minister; being in service to community by serving meals at a Portland transition home spoke to him. Although he never said it, I'm certain he felt grateful for his own recovery, particularly in those moments among many who too struggled with addiction. It was a gift to all of us that this minister was able to share a memory of Dad also, seven years after his death at Mom's memorial. I smile when I remember his reaction when things got a bit "woo woo" for him during those church services. If opened with greeting others in the congregation during the "Welcome Song," Dad would stand up, give me his flippant smile, shake his head, cross his arms, and say, "You know I don't do this."

Late in the 1960s Mom had a falling-out with our beloved grandmother that changed everything. Mom already suspected that this mother-in-law had her own drinking problem, enabling her son to drink during their shared social time, living nearly next door. On this day, my slightly intoxicated grandmother accused our mother of being permissive and careless with us kids, advising her to quit her extra activities to remain home with her children. Our mom was uncomfortable wading into the social class she married into, and this mother-in-law had graciously first welcomed her in. Now she felt abandoned and as if she might have an emotional breakdown. Mom felt shame for not being the perfect housekeeper or wife her husband could come home to and share a drink with. Upon learning that her mother-in-law was giving Dad phenobarbital pills to help him feel better, Mom pleaded with her to understand the dangers of mixing them with alcohol.

Mom's father sided with her mother-in-law, further isolating her. Although he had warned this daughter upon her engagement that this man came from a different part of society, these years further into marriage he agreed she should stay home and take care of her family. He asserted further that she carried the blame for their marriage challenges. And maybe the final lynchpin for our mom was when our newer progressive and trusted priest agreed.

Mom initiated counseling sessions and was terrified she had lost faith in God. She straddled two worlds, that of loving mother and fearful, terrified wife. In her memoir, written decades after the experience she wrote:

> My children kept me sane, with their "normal" lives of school, friends, sports, roaming the nearby fields and woods. In making sense of this experience, I realize it was truly the age-old transition between youth, innocence, and illusions of "living happily ever after," and the necessary breaking away from dependence on parents in order to move into adulthood. I was, after all, thirty-three—wasn't that the predictable time for a mid-life crisis in those old days? As difficult as it was, I felt enormously brave to confront this powerful, previously idolized mother figure and my own father. I also had to confront my deep need to be loved and approved of, as I had no feeling of who "I" was beyond wife and mother.

However, when it happened, Patty struggled and her faith dissipated. She straddled the traditional world of the Christian Church with Al-Anon's higher power messaging, and the world of Eastern philosophy, meditation, and mind-body healing. She felt alone as therapists and priests she sought for support didn't seem to understand or recognize alcoholism's impact on a spouse. Her pages but not my memory inform me of the excursion she made to Lady of Peace Retreat Catholic Retreat House in Tacoma, leaving us in the care of an older cousin. Patty walked, prayed, and talked to a priest as she attempted to "will to will the will of God."

Not long after that, in 1969, threat of physical violence made Mom feel she had to protect us and herself from our drunken father, and she filed for divorce. Our dad was known for being the funny guy when he was drunk around friends: when he stopped drinking a few even argued with him that he didn't have a problem. I don't remember knowing anything then of her fear of physical violence, I just knew they argued after he returned late on some weeknights and I would hear Mom slam the front door on her way out on a walk. My older brothers and I can't imagine ever fearing that our dad would physically hurt any of us: and yet we understand how differently anger, pain, and fear appear in an intimate relationship. Mom protected us as much as she could, I understand now. I was in the fourth grade and today understand why my classroom teacher then, about whom I wrote in *My Music Man* and later modeled a book character after, was important to me that year. Although our parents lived apart for six months, they temporarily repaired their marriage.

The next lifeline came by way of a dream job offer for Dad as editor and publisher of the *LaGrande Observer* in 1972, with the demand that he commit to sobriety before accepting the job. Mom further insisted he be sober a year before we joined him. Although my oldest brother decided to move with Dad to begin high school, the rest of us finished our school year and we were able to sell our house before moving over. In a short time, exploring Oregon's eastern part wowed us as we hiked into snow-topped Wallowas and experienced more extreme seasons in our pillow-topped Grand Ronde Valley. LaGrande and Eastern Oregon was a haven for all of us even if it lasted less than two years: Dad was unexpectedly fired by the newspaper owner. Dad had remained sober those LaGrande years: drinking had nothing to do with the firing.

Our return to Portland from LaGrande was difficult on us. Not long after our dad began drinking, flooded by financial panic, he took the job he could readily find in advertising. While he did eventually go on to find sobriety, in the decade since I first wrote about Dad's recovery, many workplaces have improved their commitment to support those with addiction. I'm grateful for his recovery; I'm sad for the lost time and damage it caused.

None of us kids felt we fit in with our Southwest Portland peers. I felt out of place surrounded by families and kids more sophisticated and well off than our family. We kids struggled in different ways; but in the end it was Mom and Dad who struggled the most with Mom divorcing Dad five years later. Mom continued to explore eastern and Native American philosophy and beliefs while completing a Master's Degree in Special Education, only to serve as an adored but burned out teacher.

It saddens me that although I have held a copy of Mom's memoir for years, I never closely read the sections of these dark times before. I was not drawn, or maybe didn't allow myself, to reach back into that darkness: I felt I knew enough from open sharing by our parents after their remarriage. Although Mom and I discussed those years, I better understand now, how hard it was for her to be the protective mother she knew she needed to be. Yet, decades later, she processed it in her own writing for herself. Maybe there were other memories better for us to share in the time we had together while she was alive.

All five of us felt our parents supported us in what we did, until the dramatic changes in their relationships precipitated trauma. We all suffered in our own ways. One of us felt he lacked the support of anyone being there for him; he simply pretended that everything was okay. A kind-hearted and charismatic kid can get away with a lot, it turns out. For me, most impacted was my relationship with Dad, as I wrote in *My Music Man*. I'm grateful to have had the nearly thirty-five years between Dad's recovery and death to talk about it all, and to find our own way to share humor in some of the retrieved memories. But I still regret I couldn't translate his attendance and support for my athletic and scholastic ventures into love for me during my teens.

I too wonder how my gender affected me in this turmoil. Being the only daughter, if there was a side to choose, I favored Mom. Our family structure influenced the close bond that Mom and I shared: I had no sisters to go to or fight with. It also influenced me to become athletically competitive. I wanted to prove my worth and the best place, it seemed, was on the sports courts. When I was seven or eight, I questioned Dad about why I was restricted by him to throwing a softball rather than the hardball, and then I went out to prove I was a better player than my younger brother. I loitered at his baseball practices until I was invited to run the bases, and although comparisons were unfair as I was older and bigger, I was still "only a girl" in those 1960s. In *My Music Man* I recount the memory of dads and boys taunting me as I batted during my only Little League season.

I was a good athlete and Title IX gave me an avenue to develop friendships with girls who shared the love of sports and competition: at a level far beyond what my mother was given, though not nearly as competitive as what my daughters of the 1990s experienced. I was a good student who loved learning and worked hard for straight As but without being as driven as Mom. Playing college ball was when I recognized the negative impact athletic competition was beginning to have on me. After being a "walk on" college volleyball player at the University of Montana and making the varsity traveling team, I chose to walk off less than two years later.

Many of the big decisions we make in life are sparked by a compelling incident. For me, quitting college volleyball had many causes, but the compelling incident was a clear memory I still have of waiting on the bench to return to play during a tournament and hoping a teammate would play poorly so I would be put back in the game. Too, our coach was verbally abusive in his quest to win, I hated missing classes to travel to games and wanted free weekends to enjoy the outdoors surrounding me. I never regretted trying out for the team nor did I regret quitting when I did.

I won't attempt to say which parent added what to the secret sauce—though Mom was more engaged in our parenting—that helped me become a kid who was confident, interested in learning, and given the opportunity to explore and enjoy independent time. The challenges my brothers and I suffered socially were mostly related to having sustained two relocations at key developmental periods. My brothers and I were all impacted by Dad's alcoholism, our parents' separation and eventual divorce. How we were impacted depended a lot on our birth order and age when the trauma hit. I'm certain family and individual therapy would have made a difference to us all, but it went largely unrecognized back then, even for our well-educated Mom. She sought marital counseling, and individual support through Al-Anon then, and maybe thought she was sparing us by not calling out counseling as an opportunity for her children. We kids simply waded through, to varying degrees of success.

Having now co-parented two daughters to adulthood, I look back on what we might have done differently. My now grown daughters recently shared their memories that they rarely saw me cry during their childhood. I wanted to push back, argue: of course I cry! Gratefully, their dad is an open weeper; crying before me in a sad movie or in frustration. I appreciate now the stereotypical reversal in our relationship but still look back at this and try not to be defensive. "Yes, Mom," said one daughter. "I remember you crying three times: after 9-11 and twice when we really frustrated you." My oldest brother remembers seeing Mom cry during childhood, but I don't. He got the brunt of knowing the tough stuff and then perhaps Mom got better at trying to protect all of us. And me? Yes, maybe I tried to shield my own kids from any sign of trauma in hopes they would not know pain, without understanding then what we know now about the importance of being open with our emotions.

I too think we silently placed more expectations on our daughters to achieve than we intended. How much of this is impacted by the society or school they are part of, their own nature, and how we as parents try to support what our kids seem to be good at? I know we were far from perfect, though we tried to avoid being helicopter parents. It probably is true that we all screw up our kids in one way or another, even when we try hard not to. I am eager to watch our daughters and partners raise children to see their take on all this.

What I am learning is how my quest to Being the Best, has not always been good for me. The writing I have undertaken during this last decade has been my biggest teacher. It is allowing me to seize the joy by doing, like in those early years of my life when I would throw the hard ball into the pitch-back net or shoot hoops for hours—not because I was trying to make a team but because it was fun. My daily mantra is to be at peace with never winning accolades for my writing, but to take joy in knowing what I write touches others in some way. And the icing on top? It allows me and others to discover more about ourselves. This is my sixties-something quest and gift.

Ghosts in the House: Making Sense of One's Life
From Patty's unpublished memoir, 2008

I HAD AN opportunity in 1995 to tour the house my husband and I lived in with the first three of our five children. This was the first time I had returned to the house where we had lived from 1957 till 1965.

Ghosts followed me around: the ghost of a young, impossibly naive, innocent, and optimistic woman trying to keep a spotless house, as the perfect wife and mother. Ghosts of two young boys jumped out everywhere: flashes of episodes in our life erupted as I toured each room: the fireplace where Andrew fell and needed stitches; the bathtub where Dede cut her chin; the family fireplace where the three-year old had peed because he was too lazy to go up to the bathroom; the door their boxer dog had chewed; the stairs where she had fallen down and sprained her ankle during the Columbus Day storm; the patio where first two, then three, then four children raucously rode tricycles, celebrated birthday parties, and created general mayhem. Yes, and the not so warm memories: standing on the step where she threw a coffeepot at her husband.

Where had she gone, this woman? Was she simply absorbed into the act of becoming a mature adult? Why could I not bridge the gap between us? Was it only the loss of innocence, the vulnerability, and the reality of forty additional years of living, with all the stress and strain upon relationships? Perhaps it was the reality of adult children, compared to the unlimited possibilities they held in their young life, the unrealistic hopes and dreams of their parents? Where had they gone?

Weeping, I stopped in the familiar-but-different kitchen. What was the sadness I was feeling? Why could I not connect with that younger woman? Heretofore, I had believed that life was a long, seamless, connected whole. There might be aberrant episodes, but life was about developing character through linear experiences, the continual act of consolidation of what one had learned. Wisdom became the application of all of that to one's life.

Suddenly, this theory felt flawed. That evening, I had an overwhelming urge to return, to take that ghost of myself into my arms and hold her, comfort her, tell her that the road ahead would be rocky. Not to be so optimistic, so trusting, so naive, or she would be deeply hurt. I wanted to protect her, to right all the wrongs she would experience. I wanted to create the actual world of possibilities she had dreamed of—no disenchantment, betrayals, and loss. The best I could do would be to live with the story and let the meaning emerge. I later decided to write a fairy tale about this experience.

Patty's Fairy Tale: A Case of Mistaken Identity

Once upon a time, not so very long ago, and in a country not so very far away, lived a woman. Wise for her years, she viewed her life as an unbroken, interconnected piece of cloth . . . long, frayed in places, yet with a consistent pattern woven into it. With great satisfaction, she viewed her sixty plus years with no regret. Oh, perhaps a few twinges of curiosity about other paths she might have taken, but nothing to cause sadness or grief.

As she sat examining the cloth that was her life, she could see the patterns that repeated, the pulling in of odd and wayward threads, but which, ultimately, created an even richer design. Occasionally she spotted knobs of thread that seemed to spoil the perfection, yet from a different perspective, she could see these imperfections only added to the overall beauty of the cloth. It was as if who she had been in all the decades of her life, though changing and growing, retained an essential wholeness and completeness.

While she was gazing at the cloth, she suddenly found herself falling into a trance. She was sucked into a vortex of energy. It was as if she were being pulled back, back, into the first quarter of her life—into the place in the cloth where the pattern was not yet apparent. Disturbed, she tried to get her bearings, to grasp something familiar and stable. Within a blink of an eye, she found herself in an old setting with a familiar but curiously unknown woman.

Who was this young woman she saw there, so bright, young, and innocent? Who were these young children, playing with such energy and joy? Why was she such a stranger, so unfamiliar? If this were a dream, surely she would have an intimation of whom the figure was. She was so hard working, her house spotless, her children flawless. Light seemed to shine in everything; not the light of wisdom earned through living a long life, but the light of innocence, potential, and possible hopes and dreams.

As she toured the scene, the woman's heart became heavy. Why could she not connect with the young woman? How had they become severed? In her trancelike state, she became more and more disturbed. Feelings of immense loss and sadness flooded her. She had a haunting feeling that she *should* remember the younger woman. She awoke from her trance. Was it a case of mistaken identity? What did it mean? Why was she weeping?

The Jungian writer, James Hillman, suggests that the seed of who you are may or not be revealed as young person, but it is there. It's about nurturing and encouraging its unfolding. It's not about adding on to oneself to "get" character or wisdom. It's about recovering, or uncovering one's basic, essential self, or Soul. How do you go about glimpsing this daimon, whose special needs direct your life toward its possibilities? You don't start with the child and her particular traumas or wounds—which was what I was doing when I first set out to write my autobiography.

Hillman suggests you start with who and what you are now in your full maturity. You look at the leaves and the fruit and then work your way back to the roots—not just "any old roots, but often the gnarled and distorted ones that gave you your unique and peculiar shape." In these gnarled roots you may find the foreshadowing of the larger, more mature and wiser person.

Often the foreshadowing is found in a symptom. Hillman suggests that in early life the daimon or angel knows the possibility for that adult life and acts to protect that possibility through symptomatic behavior so that it may fulfill or reveal itself when circumstances are most propitious.

John O'Donohue, in *Anam Cara*, suggested that the future of every experience is its disappearance. In his book about soul love, he asked a fascinating question: Is there a place where our vanished days secretly gather? Where does the light go when the candle is blown out? "The name of that place is memory." What was not significant about my earlier self was the innocence and trust, but the incredible ability to love deeply and with great compassion . . . positive outlook, generosity of spirit, ability to forgive.

My Memoir is a making-sense of my memories, forged through seventy-three years of living and loving, forgiving and forgetting, and through it all, acquiring wisdom and the willingness to rediscover my lost innocence and trust. Later, reading *Thirteen Moons* by Charles Frazier, I was moved by the author's reflection on Native American philosophy regarding memory. They relied on the oral tradition for generations because they believed that once a story was written down, it became rigid and was no longer a living, integral part of the tapestry of one's life. I see that in doing just that, I have imprinted my words in perpetuity, knowing that as the years pass I will continue to recall and relate events from an entirely different perspective. That is the risk one takes in writing memoirs.

Thank you wise mother for sharing your then seventy-three-year-old thoughts to those of us younger; still naïve, hurt, or stuck in trauma. By writing your journey and your views back then, you help remind us that perceptions of life's details change with each new moon. And that's okay.

Midlife: Thoughts Then and Now

WHEN I WAS TWENTY-SIX years old my fifty-four-year-old mom received her doctorate. I had completed my master's degree one year earlier in Seattle and Mom divorced our dad seven years earlier, after being married for nearly three decades. When she moved from Portland to San Francisco to enroll in graduate school, some of her friends were appalled. These women like her who had married straight out of college were immersed in the lives they felt expected of them, even if in quiet moments some of them questioned why they had to give up so much of themselves in the process.

Our parents' mutual friends walked the slippery slope of supporting these new divorcees. Mom and Dad were gracious and fortunate that none of their close friends chose sides. When Mom left the marriage, my two teen brothers were still at home while my older brothers and I were ensconced in post high school lives, me a college sophomore at the University of Montana. The night I received the call with both of them on the line to announce their divorce I gripped the corded rotary phone and thought I might vomit.

I didn't know then that when Mom returned to Portland State University to receive her Master's Degree in Special Education when I was in high school, she felt compelled to address deep fears that she may need to support herself in the future. As she did with most everything in life, she threw herself into teaching, focusing on those who were at the time tagged emotionally handicapped: often visiting parents and families outside of her normal classroom time, some without the capacity to support their children. She cared deeply about these kids. Today, we might say she felt morally distressed.

When I was a high school senior, I knew she was having hot flashes but didn't know she too lost hope for her marriage even with the support of counseling and Al-Anon. I didn't know at the time how much the women's movement affected her next decision.

. . . A background noise that unconsciously collided with the limitations placed upon women of the fifties: Work hard in college, make friends, so you can be a helpmate to your husband; oh, and you might need a job if your marriage doesn't work out. No thought was given to personal fulfillment, expansion of our selves, and our boundaries. Too busy to be involved politically during the seventies, I gradually expanded my involvement in community affairs which appeared threatening to Dick. In December I took the final step in dissolution of our marriage by filing for divorce.

All of us kids were stunned, but my youngest, then high school-aged brothers were most impacted. Mom suffered enormous guilt in leaving her children, later writing a letter to one of her sons explaining the decision and her regrets. Mom moved into an apartment a few blocks away, and however difficult it was to do so, my parents jointly attended their sons' sporting events and graduations. Shortly after, Dad rebounded into marriage with a woman he met through Alcoholics Anonymous, even though when he first stopped drinking after Mom moved out he refused AA support. Life in this household for my youngest brother still at home, a house that once belonged to our grandparents within blocks of Portland's nature-laden Washington Park, morphed to include Dad's new wife and her three children.

Our mom took on this new chapter and pursued work, friendships, long backpacks, and intimate relationships that were alcohol free. In 1984 after all five children had flown the coop, Mom made her big leap to move in with a sister in Novato, California and begin classes at the California Institute of Integral Studies. She used her divorce settlement to finance graduate school, and soon found her own apartment in San Francisco.

I took huge risks and grew intellectually and spiritually. Somehow this dissolved some of my confusion and mystery regarding what those rejected terms—God, Divine, Spirit— really meant. I began to further question all of my beliefs, my idea of faith, good and evil, and look for answers outside the framework of established religions. I have never ceased

questioning, yet I found some contentment in being willing
to live within the questions.

Mom's favorite class was Sanskrit. Her least favorite was
Psychopathology: she disliked labeling disease and yearned for a more
philosophical, spiritual approach to understanding people's problems.
She changed majors into the East-West Psychology Program and
signed up for the next semester's five-month study-travel program
to India, Nepal, Thailand, Hong Kong, and Japan, where she would
live with host families and study the birthplaces of the five major
Asian religions. In her five months at CIIS before the trip, she slept,
lived, and breathed questions surrounding faith, belief, humanity's
one-ness, and the deeper intricacies of interpersonal relationships.
Soon after, Mom traveled out of North American for the first time to
Asia with her fellow mostly twenty-something students.

In Mom's final year of life, she delighted to hear me read her
journal entries from this trip. I understood then how my reading
of these archived stories allowed her to relive times her working
memory had begun to forget. The trip was life changing. In New
Delhi she explored nearby holy cities and passed wandering cows and
pigs, monkeys perched on walls and roofs, and smelly open sewers
on either side of the lane. She experienced a state of transcendence
visiting the inner chamber of Taj Mahal and Gandhi's Tomb. Her
journal details the deep connection she developed with each host
family as she continued on to Jaipur and Benares. In Kathmandu,
living with a family of five small boys, she was given a bucket of
cold water for bathing and wondered what she might do with her
life when she returned to the states. She wanted to adopt each child
she saw begging on the streets. Mom met with Buddhist monks and
trekked for five days high into the mountains; not allowed to trek
with women alone, her group hired a guide and porter. Mom was
energized by new mountains that differ from the Cascades she knew
so well.

The storm is blowing over and we walked out to see
the mountains with a fresh coat of snow at 8000 feet,
clouds billowing around the nearly 26,000 foot peaks. It's

overwhelming. My adrenaline was running high, and being able to be one with the villagers was an honor. Spring is beginning and we saw fields of bright yellow mustard, flowering cherry, and apple trees and, wonder of wonders, fifty feet rhododendron trees with bright red flowers.

Later, Mom heard from her host family.

Patty, you became one of our family members who appeared as a new leaf of life or light, who reflects the solace of human mind. In fact, all of our children did not know their own grandparents. So, they couldn't receive any affection from them. In that long period of time, they feel happy to enjoy with you—regarded as a "grandmother" wholeheartedly. On the other hand, we also find you as an ever faring friend. You, therefore, won victory not only for your country but for all human beings and minds.

Mom continued onward to Bangkok and nearby villages where she connected deeply with people of the Thai Hill Tribes. Her group suffered their most chaotic and frightening day when their truck was involved in an accident *en route* to Chiang Mai. Many of her fellow students required hospital attention, though in the end everyone was okay. Mom felt responsible as the eldest of both students and professors, feeling in retrospect she should have ensured they had safer transportation. And yet, she traveled onward to Hong Kong, Canton, and Kyoto. Even in the midst of all of it, she felt bogged down by her required project papers. Upon her return to California, her elation became clouded by incessant questions as to what her dissertation topic might be.

I began graduate school in Seattle the same year Mom began her program in San Francisco. Dad's new wife complained to him when I took a blanket of my grandmother's out of the family closet, a house I lived in through high school while making daily visits to my grandmother in her nearby apartment. Dad solidly stood up for me. I was angry over what felt like jealously mired with stinginess: how did his new partner not understand the grief I still felt for this beloved grandmother who had died only a few years before? Although I was becoming closer to Dad in his sobriety, his wife's presence encouraged me to stay away.

As my parents sought their own independence and next steps, I too struggled to find mine. I did well at school, spent most of my time studying and serving as a research assistant where I weighed filters invisibly coated with arsenic and lead from the recently shuttered Ruston ASARCO smelter. I took long solo walks to Seattle's Pike Street Market, treating myself to coffee and a muffin on a rare Saturday as I stared out into Puget Sound; not knowing three decades later I would use this scene in a published novel. Yet, I too struggled to figure out what to do about my longtime now distant intimate relationship: I worried I wasn't ready to settle down with one person. Subconsciously, my worries were prompted by my parents' story. It took me and my now spouse a difficult year to figure it out. Although always close to my parents, our landline calls happened less often.

Before classes started in her third year at CIIS, Mom spent time with all of us in Portland, and unexpectedly with our dad. She felt in a different space than before and they comfortably caught up on things: us kids, their lives, and activities. The two of them always felt, although they were divorced from each other, they were still parents together. After lunch, the two went out on Dad's boat the *Walrus*: nostalgic along the Willamette. A river central to their co-raising of children.

> I felt the need to discuss an experience we had in 1966 that we had never been able to talk about. I wanted him to hear my version of it, and I needed desperately for it to be acknowledged for the first time. I went through the story with tears in my eyes. He listened quietly. I felt uneven, emotional, and vulnerable. Then, he made a quiet statement where he was in life then: not in defense, just another perspective. Suddenly, unexpectedly, I lunged into the worst episode of our marriage, trying to help him see that had he responded in a loving, understanding way, it might have created an opening for entirely different actions. Again, he quietly, without any defensive comments, then gently reaching over, put his hand on top of mine and said quietly, "Yes, I know."

We didn't speak for a long time. I was too close to a real outpouring of tears. I felt a confusion of being deeply moved, tinged with sadness and regret, and ultimately, relief. When we said goodbye, he put his arms around my shoulder and said, "You know I will always care about you. Take care." It was nice to be friends again.

As Mom returned to San Francisco, though continuing to Oregon and Montana during the next couple of years for visits with kids and friends, she settled on her dissertation topic. The seed of an idea planted by her own life and those of her Asian women friends led to her final dissertation question: What was the experience of a critical event or crisis point which led to a dramatic midlife career change?

Our dad divorced his second wife in 1986: he was gentle and financially generous in their settlement. He had come to recognize how he had rebounded into a relationship as he grappled with his need to provide for others after Mom's initiated divorce. I finished my master's degree that year, and Dad and I created a new, honest relationship: in my heart I knew he had done the work on his path to sobriety.

As Mom toiled through her doctorate she followed up on a commitment she made after completing Werner Erhardts' "Six-Day Course" to clean up her most damaged relationship. My brother was then involved in Scientology and offered a Scientologist Chaplain to mediate the session. Without judgement, our parents entered into this two-hour face-to-face session with this skinny, chain-smoking but skillful mediator. Afterward, Mom and Dad took a long walk on the cliffs above the ocean and shared dinner before he flew back that evening to Portland. They felt clean, clear, and recognized the re-kindling of a deep friendship.

The next year, Mom traveled to see us kids: she was guided by a need to be with us during the August "Harmonic Conversion," an event she and others anticipated as a planetary shift in consciousness. She stopped by Dad's apartment to see my visiting brother.

When the door opened, Dick stepped out in a beam of radiant golden light. The past and future dissolved, and we were in the present moment, loving each other more deeply than ever before. It was the Dick I fell in love with in 1955, then a "golden boy."

I realized then that deep inside we had experienced each other at the soul level, but that alcoholism and my response of anger and co-dependence dimmed the light for both of us. Neither of us was able to remember who we were at the deepest levels, and the loss grew greater as the years passed by. Our bond deepened, strengthened by the growth we made separately during those past eight years. We were given the gift of forgiveness and acceptance and moved forward and upward toward a different kind of sobriety.

It's a funny thing how differently us kids reacted when our parents got back together. When they first broke up, each of us might have given anything to have them happily remarried. And yet, in time, we developed our own worries. I was thrilled and believed I had seen it coming; but some of my brothers either couldn't let go of the trauma suffered during the breakup, or were protective of one of them getting hurt. Years later after Dad's death, the Boston Globe Love Letters podcast featured our parents' story, the host reminding us that our parents joined a tiny minority of divorced couples who remarry each other.

A few years later Mom not only remarried this first and only husband, but was a favorite college adjunct professor at Marylhurst College, a non-traditional Oregon institution that didn't seem bothered then, like some other universities, that her psychology degree was non-clinical. Mom specialized in courses that especially attracted women at mid-life. A few years later when I was busy with my own career and raising two young daughters, she published the book, *Mythmaking: Heal Your Past, Claim Your Future.* Mom's teaching was interrupted not long after and before she was ready to retire when she was diagnosed with an autoimmune illness.

Late in her life I finally cracked open the doctoral dissertation she published that June, 1988. She and Dad had remarried a few weeks later among the blooming roses of Portland's Washington Park. Only a few blocks away from the house that held memories of those difficult marital years during my high school years, and striking distance from their newly shared apartment. Few kids get the chance to attend their parents' wedding as adults. Although only a coincidence, my long-time boyfriend and I finally tied our knot later that fall, marrying at the home of their dearest friends from long ago: friends that held tight to support them both during their years apart.

I had come across the dissertation while helping Mom downsize again, before her final, unknown to me at the time, move into my home. The title of the tome astounded me: "*The Experience of a Critical Event Leading to Dramatic Midlife Career Change for Women—A Phenomenological Investigation.*" How had I not known or remembered the details of this lengthy document, I wondered then? Might it be akin to our second reading of a book later in life, time and experience influencing its impact on us?

This dissertation presents the findings of an existential-phenomenological investigation into the experience of a critical event leading to dramatic midlife career change for women. Six women were solicited and each was interviewed twice. The first interview began with a request by the researcher framed as: "Can you tell me about an experience of a critical event or crisis point which led to a dramatic change at midlife?" The second interview further explored and elaborated the experiences described in the first interview. All interviews were tape recorded and transcribed.

Transcripts of the interview were then explicated using both a hermeneutical interpretative read of the texts and Husserl's method of free phantasy variation to reveal the essential meaning-structure of a critical event. It was found by this researcher that this experience means that, whether there is a disquiet that starts inside or an event that happens outside, one begins to hold oneself as the agency of meaning in one's life. One confronts death, seeing that if the life which has been built has ended, then the living can end. One is forced to figure out what is the real meaning in one's life, and how to live it out according to new values and changed perceptions. In this process, a critical point occurs at which control is surrendered, and one accepts responsibility for one's life experiences. An event then presents itself which offers freedom, new choices, and dramatically alters the direction of one's life.

Later in the work, Patty explains how the germination for her research took place three years prior as she wrote her paper, "Role Conflicts in Asian Women's Lives," during her travel/study program in Asia. She became deeply involved in personal relationships with five women from three different countries, India, Nepal, and Hong Kong, in whose homes she lived for a month at a time. Rather than the women becoming research subjects, they became co-researchers as together they explored the experience of being a woman in different cultures. Patty wrote how their stories—"poignant and unyielding in their statements about life in a patriarchal society"—moved her to continue research on women's lives and opened the possibility of this project.

The research profoundly impacted her. While she was intrigued at the beginning by her own interpretation of her journey, she became quickly engrossed with the intense stories of dozens of other women. Knowing all this now helps me continue to understand the deep love so many women had for Patty, as a friend, witness, colleague, and teacher.

I grew to love and appreciate women in a new way for their courage in the face of cultural devaluation and the attempt to balance issues of career and relationships. I grew, also, to appreciate my own path more deeply. Finding that I do my own share of devaluing who I am, what I bring into this lifetime, and how I express my talents. I paradoxically discovered, in the strengths of other women, my own strengths mirrored back. I was surprised to find myself a role model for younger women, particularly those at the critical forty-year junction.

Although Mom was always a model for me, I was troubled by the lack of like-minded females accessible in my age group, until I got to college. Often, older women were models for me as I stepped away from boundaries that felt rigid in my teens. And yet, differently than for Mom and her generation, when I had my own children, it was anticipated that many of us would continue working. My parents always staunchly supported my career. On-site childcares were built; I was granted six months maternity leave with the opportunity to return part-time if I chose. It wasn't easy, and now many of us women were expected to do it all. My daughters' generation understand the need to work if those babies come merely to stay afloat in today's expensive world if nothing else; many weigh the choice of unaffordable daycare with giving up a career. Choices are different than in my mom's time, and not always easier.

> The interview process was for me the most intense and rewarding part of the process. Gaining the trust of my co-researchers, and listening while they shared their profound journeys, filled me with appreciation and awe. I have a sense that the experience changed us all.

This was where the seed began to shape for Patty's idea of offering seminars for women in transition after her graduation. She felt she had found her calling. Mom knew what she wanted to do when she grew up.

When Patty turned fifty-five she realized she had completed twenty years of midlife transition and found herself at a profound turning point. She created a meditative ritual with two close friends at a quiet, secret pool below a rushing stream and performed a ritual for her passage into what she termed "later midlife" or what some Indigenous Peoples may call Circle of Elders or Circle of Grandmothers. She was exhilarated and found it her rite of passage into her next cycle of life.

Patty also wrote that the most healing event for her was reunion with our dad and the plans they made to remarry. Her dissertation quotes a statement she made in her original interview.

> Even now, I would still like to be married to the man who is the father of my children. I'd love to be going into my mid-fifties, into my older years, with a husband—the father of my children. I'd love to share my grandchildren, have family gatherings. It really pulls me. So that's the failure.

I'm teary. To have witnessed the veering of my parents' midlife journeys first apart, and then reconnected through healthy growth together and for the end of their days on earth feels a miracle.

Patty's final statement reflects on the sense of discovery she had regarding midlife women and their emergence into their own power. She shares her conviction that women at midlife can powerfully influence all levels of our systems by integrating masculine and feminine qualities which can result in planetary healing.

While Mom's abrupt jump into her next life change followed a divorce that ended her decades-long marriage, my own soul-encompassing mid-life crisis and invitation to change came with the death of my dad, now nearly a decade ago. I grieved while also acknowledging the beautiful, long life he led. *All I could do was write.* I wrote early in the morning and late at night, during my bus commute to my day job, and in my brain when on foot or bicycle. Patty's final statement today stuns me, as I reflect on the beginnings of own mid-life journey as I discovered power and creativity in writing. My journey culminated only last year as I made a significant job change, one that caused me great stress until after when I realized the wise choice I had made. I feel bold as I recognize how anger— an emotion that frightened me for much of my early life—can be powerful to compel us to make change.

Elliot Jaques, the Canadian psychologist credited with coining the term "midlife crisis," referred to it as a "time when adults reckon with their own mortality and remaining years of productive life." And while some may not characterize their experience as a crisis, they may yet encounter challenges to mental health and well-being, including feelings of distress, depression, and anxiety. Some, like me, look to newfound or uncovered creativity to write or otherwise work through trauma, births, and deaths, and changes in loss of health or ability.

While we might acknowledge our own midlife crisis, might it be healthier to imagine it as a new potential opportunity? Even if accompanied by sorrow and loss? *Whatever* that loss might be: a death, in my case driving me inward to storytelling, or a divorce, in my mom's case, or loss of job, loss of child, loss or change of health. Yes, we are mortal. The time is now to do what it is our soul seeks. We must also grieve and sit with our sorrow as we contemplate what else might come from it. To expand who we are, what we are doing here, and what or who we might become. Maybe even to allow us to climb out of whatever bad fairy tale has consumed us to age into a new view filled with challenge, acceptance, and contentment.

Mythmaking: The Power of Story

WHILE SERVING AS adjunct faculty at Marylhurst University, Patty began to write a book. Some of the content for this work came from a favorite class she taught at Marylhurst. *Mythmaking: Heal Your Path, Claim Your Future* was published by Sibyl Publishing in 1994, a publishing company begun by her sister. This occurred two weeks after my youngest daughter and Patty's second grandchild was born. It was around this time that Patty was diagnosed with chronic fatigue syndrome. Although copies of this book can still be tracked down thanks to Amazon, it didn't sell many copies. Mom shared stories with me about pitching it to disinterested shoppers shuffling through Clackamas Town Center. Yet, the classes she taught and her encouragement for other women to write their new fairy tales or myths, spoke to many. Today, I find her book profound.

Mythmaking: Heal Your Path, Claim Your Future
Introduction

Stories shape our lives. When we were young girls, many of us devoured the old myths, legends, and fairy tales. We searched for stories that would inspire and guide us into adulthood. We loved Cinderella, Beauty and the Beast, Snow White and the Seven Dwarfs, and all the others that not only entertained us but defined our roles and expectations. The stories were threads that connected us to the images, to the culture we share, and to each other.

At midlife, when we get together with women friends, we still find ourselves instinctively connecting through stories. We tell each other tales of childhood and adolescent experiences, we share current anecdotes, and we talk about the patterns that have formed through the years. Telling personal stories can be profoundly moving and meaningful, and to hear another woman's story is often inspiring.

In an earlier day, families and communities gathered to hear stories that passed on traditions and values and provided community identity. Women's lives were generally based on the expectations of their parents and their parents before them, expectations expressed in stories that usually carried a single theme: find your prince and live happily ever after.

Myths are tales that explain the meaning and goals of our lives. In the late twentieth century, we are finding that former myths no longer apply and old methods of living are outdated and unusable. The stories that may have provided guidance and comfort in generations past do not help us deal with the massive changes and the seeming chaos in our culture. We need new myths.

Today, stories are emerging that offer exciting new perspectives; they reflect and are relevant to women's changing lives. Often, when we go through a crisis, we turn to other stories of contemporary women to show us how to cope, to survive, and to prevail. We are hungry for the stories that reveal our strength, and our wisdom, that teach us how to be the heroes on life's journey, rather than the victims. And after we hear the stories and recognize our common struggles and goals, it's with a deep sense of relief that we discover we are not alone on the path.

Many of these new myths have a sacred dimension. As we share them with others, we find that we experience not only a strong sense of ourselves and our places in the world, but we connect with something greater than ourselves—a universal energy. We learn, finally, that there is healing and transformative power in myth, symbol, and metaphor. But we cannot know that power until we tell our stories.

I discovered the transformative power of storytelling in 1986 when, as part of my doctoral research, I interviewed women who were undergoing midlife career change. I had a very personal interest in midlife change; at the age of fifty-two, I had left my home and a tenured teaching career to move to another state and pursue a doctoral degree.

For the research, my interview question was, "What was the critical event or crisis point that led to a dramatic midlife career change?" The experiences of telling her story was profoundly moving for each of the women I interviewed. Several spoke of being a "heroine" on life's journey. As a result of the responses, I began to look for literature that would shed light on the power of stories and myths for women. I also began to see the midlife years—usually beginning somewhere in the mid-thirties as a period when we pursue a deeper inner sense of ourselves.

This led me to design college classes for women that allowed time for stories to emerge in written and oral form, as well as through creative projects. The power of my classes stemmed from women sharing their stories and then finding meaning in the themes that emerged. Something magical happened. The process and the sharing validated their life experiences, struggles, and questions and gave each of them a focus as they faced current dilemmas and decisions in their lives.

I was stunned by the impact on other students as I read some of the stories aloud in succeeding classes. Emotional responses included relief, surprise, sadness, pleasure, as each listener identified with some aspect of the story. One story, in particular, "The Lost Purr," generated strong reactions: silence, at first, and then an emotional outburst, "This is my life!" The listeners felt some part of them, their "purr," was lost somehow in the tug and pull of daily living and accommodating others.

We begin to heal through our stories. Because my goal as a teacher is to promote healing and transformative change for women, I was confident that a book containing these stories could also contribute to the shaping of a new cultural mythology for women.

Rollo May, the great psychologist, says, "A myth is a way of making sense in a senseless world ... Myths are like the beams in a house; not exposed to outside view, they are the structure which holds the house together so people can live in it." This is what we are looking for today: structures that will hold our houses together.

This book explores the process of building such structures, as we discover the myths, messages, and stories that shape us. By perceiving the meaning behind our choices and actions, we reveal patterns that we may see as limiting, unfulfilling, and in need of change. Storytelling can open new paths.

The intent is to inspire you to examine your own life patterns so that you may write the myth of your life. In the process, you may awaken to parts of yourself that are waiting to be expressed. Your discoveries may lead you to make different choices in life, or they may not. Either way, you will find yourself with a new perspective on the meaning of your life.

. . . It is my hope that these stories, along with the process of writing your myth, in changing yourself, you will join others in changing the world . . . We're reaffirming the value of the feminine and emerging triumphantly in wholeness. This is our collective quest.

Women and New Stories:
So Good, Patty's Fairy Tale

ONCE UPON A time, a little girl was born to a poor family on the edge of a big town. Times were very hard for them, especially for the father who now had six other mouths to feed; his wife and five daughters. The little girl, named So Good, learned quickly how to stand out and be special; she was very, very good, and she smiled even when she was not happy. Neglected by her mother, So Good tried very hard to win her father's heart by doing everything he asked of her. She worked so hard she sometimes forgot how to play.

When So Good grew up, she met a beautiful golden Prince who put her under his spell. Charmed, she left the life that was familiar and moved far away to the Princes' estate in the hills, lulled by the "happily ever after" stories.

There she was also charmed by the beautiful Queen, the Prince's mother. Young, naïve, and trusting, So Good lived a happy life for many years. When nagging fears and doubts told her something was wrong, she pushed them aside and dedicated herself more strongly to state duties: her charming husband, and their children—the four young princes and the little princess. She pretended that she was very happy as a dutiful wife and daughter-in-law.

One day she had a dream, warning her of terrible things to befall her. Soon after, the Prince was stricken with a dreaded disease whose name was never to be mentioned. The Royal Family, especially the Queen, turned cold and harsh. So Good was banished to the outer edge of the estate, and the Prince spent his time at court with the Queen and King.

Remembering her dream, So Good decided to break the evil spell of the Queen and remove herself from her powers. Distraught as she realized that she would not live Happily Ever After, and yet fearing for her own life and sanity, she ran far away, leaving her children and the Royal Family. Besieged with guilt and loneliness, she began a new life in a new country. She worked diligently to achieve success, and she learned to slay some of the dragons that threatened her.

A few years later, the Royal Queen and King died, and the Prince, now the King, finally managed to slay his dragon, the unnamed and dreaded disease. He went in search of So Good. After searching, they came together bathed in golden light, and they happily joined their lives once more. But after a while, So Good began to feel that she was falling into a deep, dark, bottomless pit. Confused and frightened, she went to a very wise woman for advice.

The wise woman told So Good that she must undergo an extremely difficult ordeal if she wished to destroy her final dragons. She would have to take a dark and dangerous trip that would endanger her body, mind, and spirit. So Good was terrified, but she knew she must take this journey alone. On her journey, she had to dive into her deepest girlhood memories, where she faced demons—shadowy, frightening figures that had stolen her light, joyful sprit, and left behind an ugly burden of guilt and shame.

Courageously she found the demons. She destroyed her fearsome burden and reclaimed her childhood innocence and beauty. She put on a magic ring her poor mother had given to her before she died, and with the help of its magic, she was able to see her mother in a different way. She could love and forgive her mother's failings. In gratitude and humility, So Good returned with a new name: Peace. She was no longer worried about Happily Ever After, but lived each moment of each day. And that was enough.

Women and New Stories: Be the Best

BE THE BEST was born into what looked to most like a perfect family. She was an Only Princess during the not-as-dark-but-still-threatening times for princesses and queens. She and her few friends pushed back against princess traditions, and the Queen adamantly supported her, sometimes wistfully. The most sensible way to push back, Be the Best learned, was to be more like the boy princes she was surrounded by in her castle and kingdom. With each passing day, she believed she related better to princes, and less and less with other traditional princesses. Together Be The Best joined these fewer More Prince-Like-Princesses as they competed alone and together in their games to mimic or beat the boy princes.

Hidden to the kingdom were nearly invisible cracks fissuring over the years into what sometimes felt an unsurmountable abyss to Be the Best's Mother. Be the Best began to sense this chasm her Mother the Queen was falling into, even if much of her childhood felt idyllic. The Queen tried unsuccessfully to hide it from her children. Be the Best didn't know how to help the Queen other than join forces with her and blame the King. Be the Best didn't then understand how difficult it was to have his only daughter turn against him, but the King tried to be a good father and to support her in her "More Like Prince Than Princess" activities. But Be the Best seemed blind to this in her protection of the Queen because she couldn't forgive the King for the disease that should not be named. She didn't yet understand how the King's disease prevented him from understanding how to help solve the family's problem.

Finally, it was time for Be the Best to move out of the Kingdom to join others on their solitary yet united journeys into adulthood. She traveled great distances and left her family behind. Be The Best took on new difficult challenges, tackling them in the way she knew to Be The Best. One day not long after, she discovered she tired of trying to be the best at her favorite things. She discovered new things and enjoyed the magic of discovery. She also found new princesses who shared her interests and beliefs and taught her for the first time that princesses didn't have to be prince-like to be different than the Traditional Princesses of the Past. She and her new Not Really Princess friends, and her Not Really Prince friends journeyed into new lands, tried new things, and met new challenges.

Eventually, Be the Best married her Not Really Prince. Together they raised two smart, curious, and kind daughters to be Not Really Princesses of the Future. They tried hard to raise these daughters in new ways, but still made mistakes. Occasionally Be the Best and the Not Really Prince didn't understand how much their own trauma unconsciously impacted their young family. They later understood this to be true with many friends.

Before Be the Best returned to her home Kingdom with her Not Really Prince, the Queen took on a momentous and frightening journey, slayed her dragon and surmounted the abyss. Simultaneously, the King journeyed to slay his dragon and was slowly healed of his disease. The King and Queen renewed their love and became important teachers for their now grown Not Really Princess Daughter and Not Really Prince sons and Future New Named grandchildren. The Princess and King renewed their understanding of each other and enjoyed their lives together, even with the challenges that can encumber aging Kings and Queens.

For many years Be the Best tried new things but she often couldn't help but still sometimes needed to Be the Best. Many years passed and the King died. A few years later the Queen too died after a very long life. Be the Best was filled with grief upon the loss of first the King, followed by the aging and death of the Queen. She missed them very much even though she was grateful for their long lives. During this near decade of grief and reflection, Be the Best had a vision that opened her heart to new creative pursuits. Through this new found creativity she felt gratitude. She endeavored to follow her heart and not her brain to identify completion and success. Be the Best understood she didn't want to die striving to still Be the Best. She changed her name to Enough is Enough. She lived out the rest of her years grateful for her new name. Enough is Enough looked with wonder into the eyes of babies, listened to the sounds of the forest, and made sure to find time to explore still water.

Our Gifts and Legacy
From Patty's memoir

BY JUNE, 2005 I was feeling well enough to serve on the planning committee for our fiftieth college reunion in Corvallis. I felt it was important to expand on the historical setting for our generation. I prepared a semi-serious thirty-minute presentation on the changes women had experienced since we left Oregon State College. Born in the depression, we bridged our parent's WWI generation and that of WWII's "Greatest Generation." Our parents grew up with jazz, light opera, silent movies, prohibition, and the Great Depression. We hit adolescence in post-war prosperity, dancing the Break and the Swing, savoring Big Band music and the Crooners. We learned to accept the Beatles and all that followed, and, thanks to our children's love of pop music, found our tastes influenced by their favorites.

We followed the voices of parents, church, culture to inform and shape us, tell us what was right and wrong, sacred and taboo. We girls were grounded, cautious, respectful, good, patient, told to have fun but not too much fun, not to be too smart or the boys might not like us; expected to find a husband in college, but have a career to fall back on. When married, we lived the Good Life of the fifties, buying homes as young marrieds, having large families, and assuming happiness and prosperity as a given.

On the other hand, many of us were so busy being mothers and wives, we felt as if the feminist movement passed us by. Now I think it had a subtle, but very influential effect on the choices we made within the first decade of marriage. Many of my friends felt restless with our restraining roles, and some turned to tranquilizers to suppress their longings, or marriage counseling. The latter, along with Al-Anon, was my path to sanity.

Something did happen to us in the sixties, as reflected in my life story. There was that first ripple of discontent (usually blamed on marriage or husband) and then the dangerous question: "Is there more than this?" Many of my friends ignored the issues, some were too absorbed to respond, and others merely shared their internal dissatisfactions with each other. I ventured out of the home teaching Head Start and kindergarten, following years of volunteer work.

Thus, the seventies issued in an age of confusion for us: new roles, increasing divorce rate, double-income families, and women focusing on "me" . . . along with the crazy beehive hairdo, A-line dresses, bell-bottom jeans, and hippie dresses. Our kids became teenagers, and many of us, stunted emotionally, began to imitate them! The ethos of the time was permissiveness, and not to concern ourselves with their littered, filthy rooms—just close the door.

We began taking time out for ourselves, leaving our husbands confused and uncertain why. These friends were our true support groups, and how we loved and appreciated each other—and exhausted each other as we spun our stories of discontent!

The eighties were the years of the Good and the Bad— the Cold War, military spending, instant gratification, awareness of the "glass ceiling" and sexual harassment, as well as a return to spirituality, the New Age, and new thought philosophy. It was also a decade of high divorce rate within my age group. Many women went back to college, to work, as an outcome of a mid-life crisis. Madelene L'Engle wrote, "It's a good thing to have the props pulled out from under us occasionally. It gives us some sense of what is rock under our feet, and what is sand."

Like any social movement, there was a backlash—a labeling of pro-active, pro-choice, pro-Self women as Femi-Nazis, at worst, or just "feminists" at best. Whereas before, working women were criticized as abandoning the family, during the later eighties, to say you're a stay-at-home mom brought raised eyebrows. We were thrilled, and initially envious, of the Title IX program for girls, delighting in the options open to our daughters and grand-daughters. I followed the pattern of those years: return to college for

Ms. Degree, career, divorce, and more education and career change. By the time that decade ended, I was re-married and happy with a newly framed relationship that afforded equality, companionship, and continuity in our long relationship.

Then the nineties—the Age of Technology—hit! Many of my friends retired or traveled all over the world with their husbands. It seemed to be a decade of returning intimacy for many long-lived couples, a reward for all the years of hard work and satisfactions gained in seeing their children launch their own lives.

Today I can read Mom's talk prefaced by pre-event anxiety. She worried the seriousness of her remarks might not match the lighter after-dinner mood. Her friend suggested she ham it up by changing hats as she moved through her description of the years: mortarboard, bridal veil, pillbox hat, beehive hair, and so forth to her final hat: a bike helmet. Even with the sideline humor, Mom's final takeaways were authentic and relevant to these friends and peers.

Even those of us who moved beyond the small circle of family and friends to do big things in the world—corporate, business—ultimately return back to that small intimate group. The place where truth and vulnerability are shared, where unconditional love is given and received. Women are relationship oriented: We pass traditions on, but it's usually the daughters who enact them for their families.

Keep passing the torch. It might be something as tangible as an old piece of silver that was your grandmother's, or a bit of wisdom passed on to a grandchild, or unconditional love to a cranky friend or a rebellious child, or an impatient partner or It might be courage—supporting someone to take a stand for them.

Being loved by others, and accepting that love is a humbling experience, because you receive that love, not by your ego, but in that deep place of the soul.

After a lifetime of following the rules and pleasing others, we figured we've earned the right to dress gaudily if we want to. One woman said, "You can tell someone is over fifty when they stop taking themselves too seriously."

The Power of the Wild

PATTY WAS AN early backpacking adopter for her gender and generation. She was initiated by her sisters and found wilderness to be a source of strength and healing. This love she has passed on to her children, grandchildren, and I predict, great-grandchildren. In her memoir, Patty identified her earliest connection to the natural world in a chapter about her childhood as she claimed an apple and chestnut tree in her backyard as her kingdom. She sat in its welcoming nooks, away from her home saturated with five sisters, and a father and mother who didn't always behave as she wished. Mom dreamed as she climbed high in these trees amid wormy apples in summer and spiny husked chestnuts in late fall.

Mom credited her father for gifting her and her sisters the love of outdoors. While he joined friends each year in John Day to camp and hunt, all four younger daughters secured scholarships to attend Camp Fire Camp Namanu on the Sandy River. Patty identified her first mystical experience in the wild while hiking on a trail there: she was deeply connected in nature even then. Patty's father hauled out his camping equipment each summer during her teenage hood, and they camped at the beach, Crater Lake, and beyond. Camping and wilderness were outside my grandmother's comfort, and she chose to stay home, likely further fracturing her marriage.

I am certain it was because of Mom's Camp Fire days she volunteered to be my leader, on top of an already full plate, when nobody else stepped up. She supported me in my chocolate-selling mission to get reduced or free attendance to weeklong summer camp at Camp Ohnalee on the Molalla River. While some volunteer moms taught us to make tile ashtrays and painted quilt squares, Mom took us outside.

Beginning in 1969, Patty organized us five kids to join two sisters' families on our summer backpacking adventures. Dad stayed home. Although they were still married then, and Dad adored day hikes in places like Forest Park, Champoeg Park, and Spirit Lake, he refused to carry a backpack. Not me. I was ecstatic on our first trip into Oregon's Jefferson Park Wilderness, absent then today's crowds and reservations. It was the first Daum Clan adventure repeated each summer in beautiful Pacific Northwest sites, one year with four Daum sisters, three uncles and upward of a dozen cousins.

One summer we were required to make a dangerous snow-covered stream crossing in the North Cascades as water crashed below us at abnormally high levels because of late snow melt. I was frightened at the crossing after hearing about a hiker who fell through and drowned. My fear was overpowered by a blissful sense of well-being as we climbed into a paradise of meadows bursting with yellow glacier lilies and red, purple, and orange paintbrush. My endorphins rushed as I glissaded down snowy glaciers on trash bags. I began to understand the treasures we sometimes secure by risk taking.

I suspect Mom loved being in the mountains more than any other place. In her last months of life I found YouTube videos of hikers on the Pacific Crest Trail and shared them on my laptop. Her vision made it difficult to fully enjoy watching, lying in her electric bed in our dining room, and she preferred me to read about hiking adventures captured in her memoir. A few times I tried to take her on guided meditations into the wilderness. She laughed weakly when I encouraged her to astrotravel back to the trail.

Our family backpacking expeditions were uncommon in those late sixties, but not as rare as Mom's mid-life determination to hike as much of the Pacific Crest Trail as she could. Unlike the more publicized attempts by some to hike it in a single, monstrously long trip, Mom completed a series of hikes over several years to fulfill this dream. Shortly after Mom moved out of our Portland house, still employed as a special education teacher, she dreamed of backpacking solo. Although independent, now as a forty-eight-year-old, she believed it might be safer to hike with a male partner and she reached out to a friend who was a school psychologist. Although their relationship was platonic, I know Dad had a hard time balancing jealously with his relief that she wouldn't be alone, even though they were nearly divorced. Mom journaled about an equally worrisome but awkwardly hilarious account of this trip. This friend wasn't entirely truthful with Mom about a health condition and probably had no idea how determined she could be to complete what she set out on.

Since I had never gone on any backpacking trips alone and had always wanted to hike along the Pacific Crest Trail, we seemed to make a good team. "John" warned me he was asthmatic, but that he really believed the trip would cure him of asthma. My journal captures the drama of our trip.

August, 1981: We took the bus, backpacks and all, to White Pass and started north on the trail. The timing was perfect because the wildflowers were blooming rampantly, and every vista was spectacular. I was in high gear, ecstatic and nearly delirious with happiness. As we approached Chinook Pass on about the fourth day, "John's" steps became slower and slower and his breathing more labored. He finally admitted that he deliberately chose not to bring his asthma medicine—a sort of "do-without, or die" approach. I was furious, dumbfounded at his stupidity, and determined not to go home. I told him to hike down to Crystal Springs, a ski area, and find a way back to Portland so I could continue. However, that night in the tent he had a terrifying seizure. My first thought was irrational: What will I do with his dead body? I then imagined stuffing him into a large garbage bag so I could string him from a tree to keep the bears away. Coming to my senses, I put a pencil between his teeth, held his head and comforted him. When he came to, he told me he had a spiritual experience, faced death, and was choosing life. He was nearly manic in his relief and joy, and I was fearful of his overreaction and conviction that he was healed.

In the morning, however, sobered and aware of the danger in continuing without medication, he agreed to go off the trail and head down to the ski lodge, which meant cruel switchbacks both ways. I went with him. His doctor was supposed to phone in a prescription to the hotel, and I had a miserable night sharing a room (sleeping on the floor) because of his coughing and wheezing. The hotel was unable to get the prescription, but "John" was so sure he was healed. I'm afraid I had little sympathy for him—just enough to force me to be at least compassionate over his condition and determination.

We started out on the trail the next day, both feeling refreshed and I, somewhat optimistic. The trail from there to Green Pass went through unbelievably beautiful country, with scene after scene of natural splendor greeting me at every turn. I was ecstatic and unstoppable. "John," however, slowed down the second day. On the third day, I told him I was going to hike alone at my own speed. We agreed upon a meeting point at the end of the day. That morning an older man and his son passed me, and we chatted briefly. Throughout the day we ended up hiking the same section of the trail together, engaging in emotionally "high" conversations in language only backpackers would understand.

By late afternoon it was starting to mist, and by dusk it was raining, so I stopped where George and his son were camping. They helped me string up a shelter while I waited for "John" (he had the tent and I the stove). When he didn't arrive by dusk, I went back to look for him, becoming more and more anxious. Several miles back I found various garments tossed aside, but no signs of "John." Picturing him, hypothermic and dehydrated, dying by the side of the road, I kept searching but in vain. I returned to camp and George and his son set up a tarp for me, then shared their dinner with me. I had a tormented, sleepless night imagining him eaten by a bear, falling off a steep cliff, or dying of a seizure with no one to comfort him. Given all that, however, I was furious with him for spoiling my trip.

In the morning, I returned to the search area and found "John" off the trail, dazed, unharmed, but cold, wet, and frightened. His water bottle was empty and he had not eaten. With my help, we hiked the ten last miles together, and, begrudgingly took a bus back to Portland where I gave him a cool goodbye.

This same summer Mom visited me as I worked for the Student Conservation Association based at Mt. Rainier National Park. The Pacific Crest Trail edges Mount Rainier National Park along the

Park's eastern boundary from Chinook Pass down to Laughingwater Creek, a mere one-eighth or so of a mile from the Three Lakes Cabin where I was posted much of the summer. Both of my then nearly divorced parents visited me separately when I was at the cabin, Dad doing the six-mile hike alone to spend the night, while Mom day hiked in with my brother and his girlfriend.

It was a dream job, mostly. I was paid lower-than-ranger wages to hike trails, remind people no dogs were allowed in the Park, and report or take care of problem conditions. I had no handheld radio but a large radio that had no reception from Three Lakes, unless I hauled it a bit up the hillside. I spent two weeks in a high fire tower during the height of the driest fire season, and Mom made a second trip into the Park from Portland to visit. We loved the opportunity to hike in the wilds together; this nature lover who first introduced me to its bounty. Together we hiked down from the fire tower, snacking on huckleberries, to a hidden lake where we jumped in for an exhilarating quick naked dip. Like Mom, I was tough and in magnificent shape, one day hiking with a friend nearly twenty-four miles. The next fall I entered the University of Montana's Wilderness and Civilization Program, beginning the term with a two-week group backpack into Montana's Rocky Mountain Front and Bob Marshall Wilderness. Mom loved hearing the stories I shared.

I experienced my own troubling event that Rainier summer unshared with either parent until years later. I have thought more about it in recent years than I did after it happened, even though I was angry then. As #MeToo stories flooded awhile back, I couldn't help but think about how, although times are different for my daughters' generation than my great-great-greats, some things hadn't changed. My twenty-one-year-old Great-Great-Great Grandmother married thirty-one days after arriving in the Oregon Country in 1840, even though she had argued against marriage with her father a few months prior in America's civilized east coast. My Great-Great Grandmother would never have been allowed to take over her father's interests in the J.K. Gill Company had she shown the desire. While I relished my opportunity to fight my way to play Little League and with my friends appreciated Title IX benefits, though then unequal, what Mom had available to her was no comparison. And while Mom's friends and ex-husband felt comforted that she included a man in her backpacking trips, our grown daughters backpacked with just each other. So much has changed; but often it feels depressingly like not enough.

Although angry when it happened that summer, I didn't have enough context yet to imagine how much angrier I would feel later. One day that nineteenth summer of mine, my older-than-my-father National Park Service supervisor insisted on joining me on my twelve-mile regular hike from Chinook Pass. I usually hiked this route one-way into or out of my cabin, matching it with the shorter six-mile hike from Ohanapecoh Ranger Station. I thought this guy was weird and didn't understand why he came along. And as he paused near a lake early on our journey from Chinook Pass, miles yet to hike along the Pacific Crest Trail—the same trail Mom hiked that summer —he alluded to how nice a back rub would feel. I ignored him and kept hiking. He continued to encourage similar suggestions throughout the long hike. I knew only he had a radio. I hiked faster, miles to go, the trail empty on this weekday. I thought of all the ways I could punch him or push him down off the trail if he insisted on pursuing me. He suggested visiting me nights at my cabin; nobody would know, he added. I wanted to say—you creep! You are older than my father!

In those moments, hiking with my supervisor tailing behind, I was ignorant of the beauty that usually spoke to me—snow-capped Rainier, wildflowers, wisps of steam from nearby St. Helens, and the whistling of marmot. When we arrived at my cabin my stony responses silently told the jerk to move on. I reported it to the Assistant Park Superintendent the next day when I returned to the ranger station—surprised I am now to not have been nervous alone that night. As far as I know, all that happened was that the Assistant Park Superintendent quietly became my new supervisor. I was disgusted then how this man of significant rank was allowed to continue his merry journey upward through the NPS. Then, I chalked it up to what happened to females; wrong, but at least it wasn't worse. My experience was less horrible than so many vulgar, devastating stories. But it stayed within my heart these years later. Above all, I was angry to have this disruption happen within my favorite of places on earth, a bit like how I imagine Mom felt with her asthmatic friend. A friend invited to make the trip safer for her, a woman.

The summer after completing the PCT stretch near Mt. Rainer, Mom planned a hike with the man she had met on the trail the previous year. She was forty-nine years old, and her nearly grown five kids between the ages of seventeen to twenty-six. Together they organized a ten-day 120-mile hike from the Columbia River to Stevens Pass. Patty's memoir allows me today to picture her and imagine how exhilarated and joyful she felt as she hiked over glassy obsidian, and crossed wild snowmelt streams and the narrow, windy Naches Pass. I feel her crushing disappointment when they had to leave the trail earlier than expected as the weather turned stormy; Mom finding a bus to return to Portland. She was determined, tough, and gutsy. I couldn't ask for more as a female role model.

That too was the year when Mom identified herself as a burned-out teacher after two weeks of undiagnosed illness. She applied for a one-year absence from the David Douglas School District and was accepted into the doctorate program at the California Institute of Integral Studies in San Francisco. Just before moving to California, she visited me in Missoula. Etched in my mind, I hope forever, is when she joined me and my now spouse on a long day hike in the Bitterroot Mountains. Mom identified Montana as a second home. Nearly four decades later, as her dementia progressed, she told me she was certain she'd lived there. After all, her father had worked for the Montana Department of Highway as a civil engineer, and before her birth was the Assistant Superintendent at Yellowstone National Park. Three of her older sisters too lived at Yellowstone, before the family moved to Portland so that her mother could be back in society and her dad could better provide stable income as an insurance agent. One year before my dad died, when Patty was eighty, my spouse and I took her and Dad on a spectacular trip to our daughter's college graduation in Missoula, followed by a final Montana-Wyoming hurrah to view spectacular views and sites of Yellowstone and Tetons. Mom exclaimed in excitement as we watched steam rising from hot springs, boiling eruptions from geysers and marveled as we peered down over the Yellowstone River waterfall.

But on this hike back in those earlier days, Russ and I stripped naked to jump into an icy alpine lake. Being naked meant nothing: we were euphoric and appreciated our bodies for what they enabled us to experience. We invited Mom to join us as part of our generation: that it was okay to share this gorgeous lake unburdened by clothing. When Russ and I provided basic care for Mom in her last months of life, as sad as we felt in some moments, we too didn't see her physical body. We knew how much it had allowed her to do; and we still had glimpses of her spirit and determination. Today it feels part of the circle of our life, precious moments shared with this amazing woman.

Patty loved getting out in nature nearly to the end, although our visits changed. In her seventies and early eighties, she used walking sticks to hike through places like Oaks Bottom and Forest Park, and later, the streets and parks of West Linn and Lake Oswego. Sticks graduated to a walker; and eventually, a wheelchair for longer treks or for final steps back to her home. Together, she and I and other family members visited most every park within a ten mile-radius of her final homes; a few we knew intimately. One trip late in the winter, none of us aware how soon COVID would change everything, Mom and I sat in my car at the Cedaroak boat landing. We sipped tea and peered out at the winter landscape of Cedar Island, alternating between quiet appreciation and sharing a memory of the times we crossed the floating bridge to hike the island. I had no idea then how COVID restrictions and Mom's decreased mobility would turn that into our last car ride together.

I credit Mom for helping to instill in me, my siblings, daughters, nieces, and nephews, our love for nature, mountains, hiking, and backpacking. After she died, my best childhood friend reminded me that it was Patty who introduced her to overnights in the wild: she and other tagalongs of mine and my siblings benefited from her exuberance and inclusion. A few years ago our daughters set out alone together on their own backpack expedition, and Patty and I felt as though we had won the jackpot. Oh, Mom. I carry you with me in my heart pocket as I wander near alpine meadows dotted with avalanche and glacier lilies, through underbrush picking ripe blackberries on Cedar Island, and breathe in the rejuvenating bliss of nature's wonders.

Mind, Body and Health

I REMEMBER MOM'S quest for good health, even from when we were kids. Although treats weren't forbidden and we ate our share of candy, soda, and junk, I distinctly remember us begging to buy sugared cereal. Sometime when I was in elementary school Mom experimented with what was hippie then, or maybe granola today: baking whole wheat flour and honey cookies. This was decades before foodies created recipes producing healthy yet tasty delicacies; Mom's so-called cookies were dense, unsweet, and nothing to savor fresh out of the oven like a batch of Toll House chocolate chip. Instead of gooey, melted chocolate dripping from each bite, we were left with heavy, dry crumbles requiring more than a glass of milk to wash down. Us kids were glad when that baking phase ended.

I was in high school when Mom became both vegetarian and jogger. I understand now how both may have been in response to her increasingly difficult marriage and workplace stressors. Jogging in nearby Washington Park or along the Pacific Ocean near Ocean Park returned her to nature. She would run up around the reservoir, and then continue along wooded Wildwood Trail, savoring solitude and feel-good hormones, as did I on my own solo runs. Her vegetarianism left my parents sometimes cooking separate dinners. When I try to remember the kitchen of my teen hood I first smell and then visualize clouds of smoke that escaped from the oven as Dad broiled his hamburger or steak. I had begun discarding my dinner meat as a child; as a teen, Dad's love affair with red meat furthered my own dislike of it and him.

I didn't know then about Mom's secret health fears. She had already experienced bouts of an incorrect diagnosis of rheumatoid arthritis, most likely mononucleosis, and persistent headaches about which an allergist told her "it seems you are allergic to your own bacteria." Mom was diagnosed with pericarditis during her last pregnancy. All this preceded her later in life autoimmune illness battles: chronic fatigue syndrome, fibromyalgia, and systemic lupus. Yet, still, she lived a long, mostly satisfying life. As she approached eighty, she asserted, tongue-in-cheek, how unfair it was that she had eaten well and exercised while Dad spent most of his not eating well and yet he stayed mostly healthy. That is until heart arrhythmia identified him a candidate for both pacemaker and defibrillator, implantation of the latter causing an infection which ultimately shortened his life.

Patty's memoir, completed in her mid-seventies, describes these health challenges with chronic fatigue, fibromyalgia, lupus, and macular degeneration in detail. The only written reference I've found to her cognitive decline are a few pieces shared with the "Honoring our Memories" class she attended in her mid-eighties, and mostly undecipherable handwritten journal entries.

Mom searched for ideas and strategies to promote good health, often experimenting with non-traditional providers and treatments. Her earliest forays into meditation included participating for a short time when we lived in LaGrande, in a faith healing group. Soon after our return to Portland, she supported me in unproven methods to improve my increasing nearsightedness. For a short time I was treated by an Indian naturopathic provider who believed I could cure my bad vision if I set my mind to it. My best childhood friend reminds me about the oddity then for me as a fourteen-year-old, adopting coffee enemas, eye exercises and walking at dawn on dew-laden grass. To this day I am heavily nearsighted.

I began to be skeptical of a few of these. After my parents remarried, a doctor trained in integrative medicine convinced Mom she was carrying a parasite from prior Asia travels: blaming non-specific symptoms mimicking those of chronic fatigue and irritable bowel syndrome. At the same time, Patty began to further restrict gluten, sugar, plants of the nightshade family, and other foods from her diet. I was skeptical about the parasite diagnosis and treatment back then, and I too worried about food restrictions as Mom was sometimes challenged to keep weight on. Mom, though, scribed in her memoir that she believed this doctor saved her life during her final teaching years at Marylhurst.

By the end of the fall quarter, my working stress increased with out-of-town seminars, retreats, and weekend seminars. I began to show signs of burnout: students with bi-polar and multiple personalities disrupting the classroom, the dysfunctional administration system, and my book on midlife hitting a publishing dead-end. Despite those negatives, I enjoyed teaching my classes with women, especially my "Mothers and Daughters" class.

Today, I wish I could sit invisibly in the back row to hear her talk about mothers and daughters. Only recently I happened onto a short description of a workshop addressing Mothers and Daughters, as I scrolled through files on an old hard drive of hers I'd stashed aside years ago. The description was from a women's conference in Alaska in 1999. I have wondered what tips this mom of mine, co-creator of a tremendous relationship with her only daughter, might advise. I might have known that it was by uncovering her own relationship with her mother that would most inform this workshop titled, "Transforming the Mother-Daughter Relationship." I suspect it was less about ours; rather our relationship benefited from what she had learned from her life, research, and especially her bond with her mother. This workshop description advises addressing unfinished business, exploring dynamics of the child's, feminist and archetypal views, and ultimately imagining a new bond beginning with the unhealed child based on understanding, forgiveness, and respect. Yes, I imagine most women could find a nugget from this to add to other life work we undertake.

Mom made one of her most difficult decisions when she stepped back from Marylhurst. Although she experienced the most joy she'd received in work, it too emptied her. She told me then how difficult it was to create boundaries with her students, some who wanted her both as a confidante and an advisor. I clearly remember an incident as she struggled to support all of her students when a transitioning woman registered for her Women at Midlife class. Several women in the class insisted on referring to her male energy being inappropriate for the class and called her out as male. Even more so, Mom regretted feeling she had missed out when my second daughter was born in 1993, she in the throes of stress and illness. To me, though, she had seemed to be a fully engaged mother and grandmother. Gratefully, a few years later and after taking charge to reduce stress and pay more attention to her own needs, Mom rebounded into good health. This continued for nearly a decade. Patty thought she would remain healthy from then on. Although paying more attention to reducing her stress and meditating daily, Mom began to follow old patterns. A few months later she was hospitalized with an undiagnosed, seemingly serious illness.

We had all recently returned from a family wedding and travel in Italy. Mom had enthusiastically joined us as we toured Tuscany's castles and museums, hiked the St. Francis Camino, and swam in the eye-popping blue of the sea of the Cinque Terra. She alone took a special granddaughter to a Rome zoo, me incredulous that this amazing grandmother wouldn't simply say "no," after all she'd too visited the Coliseum, Vatican, and other landmark sites.

Upon her return to Portland, Mom served as chair of her condo Facilities Committee during a contentious special repair assessment, rife with personal attacks from a minority of angry residents. She began to feel exhausted again in 2004 and slept poorly. During our annual beach family reunion, after gardening in the sun, Mom fell into a bed-bound delirium of dizzy achiness, soon developing a severe rash on her trunk, face, and arms. It was the first time I self-identified as Mom's chief caregiver. I was frightened and felt responsible. Looking back now, I remember that Mom looked as aged and ill in those moments as she ever looked twenty-one years later at death. I was able to phone her primary care physician, and he advised me to give Tylenol time to take effect first. I worried he didn't understand how ill she was, and wondered if we should try to get her to the hospital, but was concerned about isolating her on the Peninsula, far from her medical providers.

I look back now and recognize how, from this moment on, I became the "go to" for my parents' medical needs. I'm not sure if it is because of my controlling tendencies, me being the only daughter, or what. Even today I remember the responsibility I felt then, and the slow building of relief as Mom showed gradual improvement over the next few days. The only time our family has driven on the beach together since my earliest childhood days clamming, was a single attempt to get Mom down to join family for our annual sand castle building extravaganza while she ailed.

Back in Portland, I was in the hospital twice until Dr. B. found a competent rheumatologist to examine me. Two weeks later, a final diagnostic test revealed I had Systemic Lupus, the probable trigger being overworking in the hot sun. Dr. T. labeled it a "catastrophic" attack, and told me I was very lucky it had not affected my internal organs, as such a dramatic attack usually does. I was put on prednisone for three months, which caused hair loss and dizziness. Dick and the children rallied around me, with Dede assuming the role of my advocate with doctors. She was unflinching in her patience with me, determined to get the best case, and showing faith in my ability to heal. I felt loved and supported in the children's concern and attention to me, yet haunted by vague yet pervasive feelings of shame and guilt: I had overdone it again. I bottomed out physically, psychologically, emotionally, and certainly spiritually. I felt I was back to Ground Zero. I had learned nothing and chastised myself for not applying my spiritual learning to my life. I moved fully into self-blame: When will I ever learn?" I whined to Someone Out There.

The next year was difficult for Mom as she worked to improve her health, while also being devastated upon the death of her oldest sister and a favorite brother-in-law. Soon after another sister was critically injured in an accident. Yet, even then, as she neared her seventy-second birthday, she was able to discontinue prednisone as her energy and blood tests both improved, and she remained on Plaquinal. Mom continued to experience improved health and energy, and a few years later found remission. She never suffered another flare, a miracle it seemed to me. I began to wonder if her case of chronic fatigue syndrome, mostly identified through a process of elimination, might have been an initial lupus flare. I reminded myself how none of that mattered anymore.

Patty believed her emotional and psychological trauma and journey impacted her physical health. I think she blamed herself for the difficulties she had throughout her life to calm anxious thoughts and slow her racing mind, especially before sleep. Mom often wondered if some of her health problems were related to hyper stress of her adrenal glands. Knowing what I do today, I wish she could have gotten a better handle on effective sleep for all those decades: it may have made a difference in her health. And yet, hindsight rarely answers questions like that.

Mom was a trouper when, at the age of eighty-three, I suggested we wean her off the nearly ten years of being prescribed an addictive sleep aid, while following detailed recommendations by her physician. I'm sorry the drug that was selected then was later found to have adverse effects following long-term use, including ties to dementia. I will admit it did help her find sleep. I understood physiological changes of aging might be impacting her metabolizing and eliminating the drug, increasing morning grogginess. Mom agreed to wean herself from it. She did experience minor withdrawal symptoms yet she acknowledged the courage leaving the drug demanded. Ironically, she never had sleep issues again. I had to force myself to stop searching the internet to deduce how these various factors may have increased her propensity for dementia.

In an attempt, perhaps, to avoid self-blame, I asked myself this question. Could a medical professional have seen what was going on, added it all up, and convinced me (or threatened me) that I absolutely had to change my lifestyle—less stress, adequate sleep, less worrying, and proper diet? It's called "self-care." Might I have avoided the final train crash? I'll never know, but perhaps others can learn from my story.

If you had asked me earlier, I did think Mom took care of herself, even if she struggled with sleep. I always thought she ate well, going through what seemed to me then crazy tests of food sensitivity, she exercised and practice yoga, meditated from mid-life on, and had a lifetime of good friends. Yet, human well-being also requires self-love and acceptance, and effective ways to deal with anxiety. We too come into this life with disease predilections difficult to know, understand, and accept. It takes courage to be willing to share our stories even knowing how stories help us now and into the future. Yes, Mom, I have learned from you. So too have your offspring and others you have touched.

I Love you Bigger Than the Sky

AS MOM NAPPED during her last months of life in our home, I scribbled notes for the book I thought I might write. I understood people graduated hospice's six months, but never believed Mom would live beyond a few. Honestly, I didn't hope for her to either. I knew she was exhausted. It turned out to be six weeks, including two of which our Willamette Valley was pummeled by a massive ice storm: our community echoed as trees cracked and crashed to the ground, severing power lines as they fell to earth. If spirits reunite somewhere in the afterworld, I'm certain Dad smartly uttered, "Patty, you always had to be the tough one!"

She who without complaint rested for eight days in her no longer electrified bed, in an unheated house warmed by hot water bottles, sleeping bags, and wool hat while we heated food by camp stove. She rolled her eyes at me when I offered, "After all, you're getting one more winter camping trip!" By phone, hospice advised me at what internal body temperature I'd need to call 911 for hospital transport. I tried to be respectful when I let the kind advice nurse understand no ambulance would be able to make it down our steep icy hill. We were grateful when our power returned and the only adverse health impact to Mom were two ugly ulcers on her lower legs where she had crossed them, hidden within the sleeping bags keeping her warm. They were just healing when she died.

After Mom died, I read Amy Bloom's *In Love: A Memoir of Love and Loss*. The next day as I pedaled through favorite places, my brain spun thoughts faster than I could keep up with. Although I had discontinued the writing I'd done during Mom's final months of life, I understood my need to write about our journey. And too, it made sense to incorporate writing I crafted during my deepest grief. I am grateful I had checked in with Mom for permission to write about her. "Of course," she told me, without hesitation. Until the end and perhaps even in the hereafter, Mom and I trust each other completely.

Mom's journey with dementia lasted about a decade, though I wouldn't have identified it that way at its beginnings. At first it was little things; repeating a question, telling a story twice. Those first several years her physician called it minor cognitive impairment, when asked. During Mom's entry into this earliest stage, Dad experienced his next round of heart issues. I was grateful, especially as I learned about challenges my friends encountered with their parents, that Mom and Dad initiated their move from multi-level condo before either of them fell down its steep stairs. My parents too were concerned about that risk and never wanted to be a burden to their children.

Mostly our parents found gratitude when life threw them a curve, especially Dad, a longtime AA Twelve Step Believer. One day prior to our helping them pack up their home, I walked in on Dad as he sat quietly in his condo basement office. He stared at his office walls, pictures lovingly arranged to depict his rich career. He was privately grieving as he prepared himself to accept this next journey gracefully. Ultimately, our parents were delighted to move into a one level, three-bedroom apartment near my home: equipped with an exercise room where Dad pedaled up to his last day. Mom joined the Adult Community Center and walked weekly for several years to a writing group where she grew new friends. One, serendipitously, had been a student in her Marylhurst class on mid-life. This group became close, trusted friends; a benefit gained when sharing writing from the heart.

When I first asked Mom for her permission to write about her, it comforted me to be able to write about this time of our life together, and her dementia. To process on paper my worries, fears, and acceptances. In my novel *Beyond the Ripples*, although character Gloria is nearly opposite of Mom during our childhood, she shares a few sentences about aging and its accompanying losses that Mom first said to me. I appreciate knowing Mom's willingness to publicly share her experiences. As Dad was public about losses and wins as he moved through recovery, both my parents inherently understood how this insider's view helps the rest of us find compassion and often better understand ourselves. Dad demonstrated this for years as he shared his recovery story to those newer to the journey. Mom shared her losses and gains of experience about her life with friends and students.

I am fortunate to understand Mom better during this latter part of her life through pieces she wrote for her writing group, such as this entry titled "Aging."

> I felt great moving into my eighties, walking daily, hiking down into Tanner Springs basin, to Safeway for groceries, (thanks to my backpack), reading a lot of books, having monthly eye injections for AMD, and talking to my sisters either by phone or through Skype. Smug no. Just grateful, and available. Last Tuesday afternoon I was sitting on an old cane chair, changing clothes, and slipped right out of the chair as if it were a pot of jelly. I scraped my arm on the bed board and realized I simply could not get up. I yelled for Dick. He gently picked me up, brought me a large bandage for my bleeding arm and put me back on the bed, where I remained for the afternoon. It upset me deeply, because I remember both parents taking falls in later life . . . Am I really that old? Always being independent and hesitating to ask for help, I am forced into it. I must remember to go slowly, using my walking sticks, and be patient, which run counter to my innate personality, and habits.

Mom worried about her memory challenges from the start. I don't recall her denying it to us, but now understand she tried to hide it at its onset. I know she felt relieved when we began to talk openly. Mom told me the hardest thing for her upon further decline, was her fear that people thought she was stupid. "You are just as intelligent as always," I would say. "But your brain has changed and it can't work like it did before." Some days she would buy that and feel relieved. As her memory worsened she worried increasingly about making mistakes. As a lifelong high achiever, her desire and innate need to do things correctly added to the stressors she felt. It was no surprise to me that she seemed to value her intelligence above nearly all else.

I recently came upon old voice mail messages from my parents. One captures Dad in his trying-to be-polite-but-urgent voice telling me the date and time for his next physical therapy appointment, hoping it might work for me to drive him. In another, an anxious Mom says she is waiting for a ride from my daughter for an outing, and she apologizes, wondering if she had the date or time wrong, which it turns out she had. Mom's voicemail message makes me sad, even though I love to hear her voice.

Several years later in 2019, as I helped downsize Mom's belongings from her assisted living apartment into an adult care home, I took time to organize and read more of her writing. This excerpt from "Losing Things" written five years prior made me realize she hadn't been as open initially with me and was more worried about her memory than I first perceived.

> I have been losing things for quite a while, but lately it has become a problem and, worse, my family knows about it. First, it was my short-term memory that began slipping. "Oh that's okay," I told myself. I will start making notes and lists and notes to help me remember. That lasted awhile, but then I started losing my lists or post it notes. My daughter, after spending time with me, encouraged me with statements like, "Mom, you're not losing it. Just think how many things we have talked about and your memory is just fine!" (My sneaky mistrusting mind says, "She doesn't really know what I am going through, and how much energy it takes to keep my calendars updated and checked.) So then I become obsessive, checking on our large-print calendar, to see what I might be missing. Sometimes I am so upset I go to bed with my covers over my head. Invariably I hear a tap on the door, and it's either my daughter or granddaughter's sunny voice, "Hi, Gaga! How's everything? Can I do anything for you?" In my heart of hearts I believe I could handle one of the two handicaps: worsening AMD or memory loss." I don't know what will happen, but I pray I won't have to play this game of charades too long or that my kids will call a family gathering to discuss "What should we do about mother?"

She and Dad shared the same internist and scheduled appointments together during Dad's final two years. I drove and listened. Mom's physical health was stellar, continuing to surprise us given her history of autoimmune illness, and Dad mostly saw cardiologists for anything medically complicated; I took him to those too. My parents' approaches to the Medicare Cognitive Assessment were from opposite camps: Dad didn't care how he did and held no worries about his memory. His memory was excellent until his death at eighty-four. Mom, however, worried about the test and even practiced ahead of time. When Dad was asked to count backward by sevens from a hundred, he kindly asked the medical assistant: You know I flunked math? (Dad was dyslexic and known to be a word guy, not a man of numbers.) That was his final answer and the assistant knew to move on. In contrast, Mom sat visibly anxious while Dad reminded us she had been a straight A student, while he was pleased to pass college with Cs.

He called me upset one night in 2014, the year he died. Mom had told him perhaps she should move into a facility because of her memory. He knew his wife worried about impacting others and felt guilty in a way that made no sense to him or me but is explained by who she was. I calmed Dad down and agreed with him that she didn't need those accommodations at this point. The solution? Mom and I visited the assisted living center next to their apartment. The previous year Mom and I toured many Portland area senior living centers before deciding that the apartment made the most sense for the two of them.

On this newest tour nearly next door, Mom liked the staff we met, the location, and the enrichment opportunities. She knew the neighborhood and would continue to be able to walk throughout it, and to Safeway and the adult community center. She commanded Dad to visit too for this backup plan. True to Dad's style, he walked over and took a solo short spin in the front room, didn't ask to speak to anyone, looked out the window at the grounds, and returned home to tell Patty it was fine. I know he felt he would hate living there but would do anything to soothe this woman he loved. Had he outlived our mom, I am certain he would have stayed in his apartment. Although I miss Dad each day and would have loved for him to live longer, I am grateful he didn't have to watch this love of his life move through later stage dementia. Among many things, I appreciate that my parents realistically planned for their futures. And although they weren't wealthy, they were both fortunate to have retirement savings and insurance to support them.

I was grateful when Mom's internist stopped giving her the prescribed memory test. He knew her well and understood the anxiety the test caused her. He was a kind and gentle doctor who had been the one to help diagnose Lupus nearly two decades earlier. Instead, he asked her to read a short article when her vision still allowed it, and to tell him about it. By then, Dad had died and Mom had chosen to move into the neighboring assisted living facility, where she was content for a number of years. What her doctor cared about most was her ability to safely get about her day, which she could. I remember how he explained it to her, by drawing a picture of a glass filled to the brim with water. Next he drew one mostly full, and explained to her that it was still a glass of water. He felt no need to refer her to a neurologist, which I believe was the right thing.

She continued to celebrate her daily often hilly two to three-mile walks, often solo when a friend or family member wasn't available. Walks and being in nature continued to fill Mom. The solo walks ended after she got mixed up on her route one day and accepted a ride home from a kind passerby. The facility called me, demanding that the time had come when Patty shouldn't go on walks alone other than to the nearby grocery store and community center. At the time I wondered if it was memory, vision, the confusing winding array of roads or collectively all three, and I was frustrated at what felt like an unfair attack on Mom. As usual, she was not infuriated, rather deeply embarrassed.

As Mom's memory declined more noticeably, at first I avoided calling it dementia, instead referring to it as memory loss. Yet, I believed I was furthering stigma by avoiding calling it what it was. I asked myself, is it because if I name it, it becomes real? Well-meaning family and friends aren't always quite sure what to say or how to behave. They want to do best, but it's easier to ignore, avoid, or pretend whatever is happening will be better tomorrow. Yes, sometimes tomorrow is a better day for those with dementia. And sometimes it isn't. And if it is, it doesn't make it like yesterday. And with dementia, maybe we think, or pray, please not me, I do all the "right" things. Yet, none of us know the entirety of the *secret sauce* for lasting good health.

I asked Mom if she thought seeing a mental health counselor might be beneficial to her; to have somebody to confide in who was not a daughter, granddaughter, or friend. She agreed and seemed to feel relieved by the suggestion. I did my research and she tried out three. This was on the heels of many successful therapy sessions Mom had arranged for herself from midlife on. The first therapist was kind, understood Mom, and she liked him. But after the second visit he told us there wasn't anything more he could do to help since she couldn't always remember what they discussed. The second I found with an organization that specialized in working with those with dementia and other brain conditions. They began with testing, the kind that freaks Mom out, telling me what I knew, she was in the "moderately cognitively impaired" spectrum. I sat in on two more sessions with the selected therapist, but pulled her out after a session when the therapist rolled her eyes at something Mom said. Maybe she thought Mom's vision was such that she couldn't see her but I was appalled. The therapist said the only treatment she could suggest was medication for anxiety and depression. At a certain point Mom did begin a low dose of medication for anxiety, but it wasn't the solution to what she needed then.

The final professional was a helpful psychiatric nurse who made house calls and loved talking with mom. She was the only professional to say what I always suspected: Mom's dementia sometimes seemed worse than it really was because of her increasingly declining vision. But we both recognized Patty was not in need of the specialized support this too-busy professional attended to. All this is to say that for our mom, social interactions and activities with her beloved children, spouses, and grandchildren, kind friends who stayed in contact, music, and trips in nature and favorite places, were the most important supports to Mom's mental health for the rest of her life. That and the power of support without judgement. I cannot thank her dearest friends enough for being there to the end: this tests and demonstrates deep compassion and friendship. It too can be difficult and disturbing for those friends who shared rich experiences earlier in life.

Although I'm not sure when Mom had her first brain scan, she had her second after she broke her hip. After she had gone through rehab and was walking again, I took her to a neurologist at OHSU, mostly to rule out hydrocephalus. Those were the days I was obsessed in finding a way to "fix" Mom's memory problems. Mom and I had a fabulous tram ride in Portland's Aerial Tram and a cup of tea at the top. Mom was told she didn't have the brain condition, and that she most likely had vascular dementia rather than Alzheimer's, although we know the two can coexist. I spent a lot of time trying to figure out why: none of her five sisters, all living into their eighties and nineties, had memory issues. I too recognized how she alone had experienced autoimmune illness, significant anxiety, and sleep struggles. I finally forced myself to accept that none of knowing that mattered then, or would "fix" dementia. Seeking poorly understood causes and solutions was exhausting me.

Most days Mom asserted she had a wonderful life. She challenged herself intellectually and remarried her life's love after he started his own path in recovery from alcoholism. They enjoyed their time together in their sixties and seventies, even with her autoimmune illnesses, traveling, hiking, and spending significant time with family. They too spent quieter social times together until his death, mid-way through his ninth decade. Mom, or Gaga to grandkids, continued to be a doting grandmother, even though her ability to engage was different as she moved into dementia than it was when her eldest grandchild was born. Sometimes I think her later stages of dementia was hardest on her oldest grandchildren who knew her as she was before. They silently grieved as they lovingly cared for her.

Once Mom referred to me as her mother. Although I knew she had suffered a tough week, I recognized an uncomfortable invitation into a new place. A different stage of life, for me—her daughter—and for her. I was confused: I thought I had already stepped well into this part of life. A stage I don't know what to call. When it happened, it upset me and I reacted, blurting out, "Mom, I'm your daughter!" She hesitated, and then answered slowly, "Oh, yes." I jumped in quickly, too quickly, in my effort to explain her statement, the one that alarmed me. "Maybe it's because I'm helping you and it feels like I'm a mother," I rationalized. And Mom agreed. Too quickly I butted in. Again. "Mom, you know I'm your daughter? Right?" I commanded, rather than asked, selfishly realizing, then at fifty-six, I still needed a mother. Yes, of course," she answered. Confident now. "But a daughter shouldn't have to take care of her mother," she added, carefully.

Mom didn't address me this way again, although she had confusion late in her journey when on hospice as I think it still sometimes seemed odd to her that I took care of her. For a while after the first time I occasionally queried her, as if to quiet the worries nagging at my belly. The exchange generated new fears for my brain then to tease through. About our future.

My reaction surprised me. Surprise that was packaged with the abrupt realization I was entering new territory. A new passage: even if I had no name for it. What is it I was inching toward, and what rite did I need to complete to ease my entrance? Why was I so surprised to be slow to recognize it? Is it because I thought I had already reached all of the recognizable milestones associated with the aging of my parents? Yet those steps were only way stations along the climb to the true summit.

The threshold to adulthood glimmers at us, repeatedly as we age. The first glistening when we move away from our parents the first time. But bah! No adult was I yet. After having my first child, a decade later? Closer, yet still I relied on parental advice: does that qualify as being an adult? Mom and Dad didn't know how to do everything and I didn't feel the need to copy their efforts—but they did provide me comfort in listening to my joy, stories, and worries. Years later, in the heart of my career—my parents were proud. They asked questions. They listened.

It wasn't until Dad died when I finally felt adult-like. His loss was more than I could fathom, unleashing words and stories urging me to publish a memoir. And it was then when I was certain! Adulthood means losing a parent. Is it because we are forced to accept that, yes, your parent has died, and, so will you? Yet it was only another step up the slope for me. Mom still offered advice, even while I helped with daily activities, or served as her eyes for the vision she was losing: connecting her with the world around her. Until the end. And now, like many friends, we are orphans. Orphaned yet grateful for decades of adulthood I shared with my parents.

As Mom's memory weakened she sometimes might ask me about my days at work, but less often offered advice. I slowly told her fewer of my problems, but instead read my stories and blogs to her. For a long time she helped me choose a right word for writing I was crafting. Her vocabulary and ability to spell stayed fluent close to the end. Then though, she would listen and might compliment me. When we were still able, we would continue to sit together by our favorite rivers and at our favorite parks, even if she traveled by wheelchair as her body tired. In her last summer she could still see enough peripherally to spot birds and flowers.

Early in the pandemic winter of 2020, we were prevented from seeing Mom in person for several months. It was one of the most difficult times in my life. I put on a smile for her as we created elaborate window musical and dance visits. We tried Facetime but mostly found it difficult. I read to her by phone while looking through the window, sometimes reminding her the blur she couldn't see was me. And I would sob as soon as I was out of view. I was grateful when I was allowed to visit Mom outside masked, and insisted I take her for a walk in her wheelchair to the next-door park. As we sat outside, my family members and I read books and played music, grateful to be with her again. And yet, the losses were tremendous. She stopped walking during our mandated separation with us unable to take her on outings. I no longer could tease her that if "you snooze you lose." She no longer could visit the parks and places she loved, and I believe, had no reason to keep doing the hard work of walking. Her dementia progressed too. I was angry and grief-stricken.

When our part of Oregon was engulfed in wildfire smoke near Labor Day of 2020, we went nearly a week without seeing Mom as the air was too unhealthy for her to be outside. For me, that was the last straw. I knew COVID infections were likely to increase in the fall and Oregon's adult care homes may again restrict visitors. I will always be appreciative of the Elder Advisor offered to me through my workplace Employee Assistance Program and my therapist who both listened closely to our story. It was in those moments that our family decided to move Mom into our house on Halloween, hiring private medical transport to get her up the steep steps of our home. Mom came in by medical transport and left just over four months later by funeral home transport. It was a decision I will always be grateful to have made.

Mom openly acknowledged her losses to me and her closest friends in her final years. She lost a good deal of her vision, required hearing aids, and may have been characterized as mid- to late-stage dementia in her last year. Dementia made Mom especially sleepy, and in her final few weeks of life she spent no more than a few hours awake, although she appeared pain free. She too felt badly for not giving back more, even though we reassured her how much she had given others through her life.

At the end Mom apologized to me for her fatigue. She acknowledged how she didn't feel she could do anything anymore: listening to books and music, visiting with family—none of that was enough for what she thought she should be able to do. She was ready to die. Family members and a few good friends joined me to remind her of her legacies, some by phone and video call as we were still in the heart of the pandemic. They told her stories of the kindness she exhibited and also shared silly memories. We told her over and over how much we loved her. On her final few days as she lay with eyes closed, one granddaughter told her by phone she was to be a great-grandmother.

I'm not sure Mom would have chosen to die if it was summer. Might she have willed herself to get out of bed and into the sun amid blossoming cherries and rhododendrons one more time? She and I never needed to say a lot when outdoors. Each time we were together in the natural world, or especially in the end as we listened to favorite music, her essence pulled itself forward. During her final week we moved her bed next to a window, icy patches remained but her being nearly shimmered in the weak winter sun. I am grateful for those last days of sun before she chose to leave us. I tried to remind myself then I was nearing our final beloved moments spent together on earth.

Throughout our Mother-Daughter Journey, I recognized and honored Mom's spirit of caring for others, sometimes at her own expense. She never wanted to be a burden, never denied her dementia, or fought our attempts to help her except three isolated times newly moved into our house when this independent woman may have felt ganged up on by two of us helping with basic care. It may have only been in the final month or two when it seemed she knew her body and spirit were simply exhausted. She had moved from not being able to doing certain things, carry on multiple tasks or actively converse, to being too exhausted to worry about any of it. And so we didn't. She listened to us read her books and passages from her memoir, we shared favorite musicals each night at dinner, but she still woke up in the morning with her beautiful smile, even thanking me occasionally, until that final week.

Patty died three weeks before her eighty-eighth birthday after five days without food and water. I'm grateful that period was short and from what we could tell, peaceful until her final rattles of death. Since those days I have traded notes with friends as they help their own parents make later life decisions. It is a common theme as many of us live longer, often with chronic health conditions and without people or financial resources during life's final chapter.

I try to practice the kindness that our parents embodied. I urge myself not to take my tasks or accomplishments too seriously. I seek ways to reduce anxiety and fear that I know never left Mom completely. I'm reminded of the friends that dropped off after Dad died, and the ones that stopped reaching out when Mom experienced dementia. I promise myself to do differently. I remind myself to take as many moments as I can to reach out to others however I can. And while sometimes we tell ourselves it is our real friends that stay with us through thick and thin, could it be that those who don't never learned how? I remind myself: Take a breath. Follow your heart. Hold a hand. Just be.

I have several of Mom's spiral notebooks I still can't let go of. They are diaries she wrote to help her remember the events of the day early in dementia, her way to seal memories. Us kids knew our mom to have nearly illegible handwriting, even when her vision was good. She wrote these later entries with extremely low vision, and they are almost impossible to decipher. I can pull out phrases like "had a lovely walk with Dede today" or "walked up to my writing group, love my friends." Maybe that's all I need to know. And while I don't believe Mom would have had the desire or courage to cut her life shorter before her memory had declined toward the end, she would have respected others who make that choice. Instead, her body and spirit did make that decision when she was absolutely done, in those final five days.

I used to think I was like my mother. Later in life I realized how much I was like Dad. Now, I clearly see bits of myself from both. I wonder who I may be more like as I age? Will I die quickly like my dad—with my mind crystal clear, but my heart worn out? Or will my physical health outlive my cognition? And what might that bring to my spouse, if he's still alive, and our daughters, or even grandchildren? Yet, what does it matter today? The sun is shining. I have a new book to write. We have other problems in our world that we all need to solve. I will get old someday, or not. I may die like my dad or like my mom or not like either of them. What I do know, is, for today, that I am grateful for all the time I spent with Mom, including her final moments. And in this moment, none of the rest of it really matters.

I try to remind myself to accept the gift to sit quietly amid the chirp of birds or whistling of the wind. Even if it isn't with Mom in my wing. I sat with Mom, she who taught me to how to be strong and independent and to believe in myself. In her final year, surreptitiously, I picked a sprig of lavender one day from a neighbors' garden, and a fragrant rose another. She laughed when I handed it to her: I learned I don't have to follow all the rules all the time. I'm learning from her experience that the time to leave behind regrets and accept what you bring to this world is sooner rather than later. To know that change is constant, and not all of it comfortable or happy. I learned to still look at this parent as a teacher, even if she did call me Mother. Our mothers will always be our mothers. Yes, Mom. I love you bigger than the sky.

Seeking Calm Waters
Letting Go

I'VE MISSED YOU every day since you died. I miss you as I walk beneath dense canopies of Douglas fir and salal; places you and I journeyed together as over time you graduated from sticks to walker to wheelchair. I miss you when I cook oatmeal and eat huckleberry ice cream, listen to All Classical 89.9, and make English Breakfast tea with a splash of milk each morning. Sometimes, in the middle of a virtual work meeting, the reflected view of our lilac dining room wallpaper stuns me back to the days you lived in this room. During late weekend strolls, the waft of a scented laundry detergent that once lingered on your clothes sets me off. Yes, everything reminds me of you. You were ready to die; we were privileged to have you in our lives to share decades together. Yet, I miss you as we do when souls special to us leave earth. This emotion of missing ripens and fluctuates each day; yes like the Jantzen Beach Big Dipper rollercoaster you once told me about.

I ride my bike on a meandering loop when there is no place I need to go. It starts out like it used to, in those before days when I'd stop by your house. When I pass Mole End Cottage, I hear your chuckle from our reading of *Wind in The Willows* during your final years. My bike drops down to River Road and I sense your excitement as the rippled Willamette River bursts into view. At the Cedaroak Boat Landing I stare across at the seasonal scape of Cedar Island, waterlogged debris hung up at the dock in the winter, cottonwood fibers collecting along the river edges in the spring. A few miles later I arrive at Willamette Park and hover near the confluence of the Tualatin River before I ride on to your favorite upriver spot to engulf your spirit with the rushing river. Each scene reminds me of you, each memory entwined into a rich patchwork. A gift you left me for as long as I can remember it.

Yes, I carry you like I knew I would, in my heart pocket. Our heart pockets carry loved ones, each in different ways: lovingly, regretfully, gingerly. My personal grief will continue morphing and circling back and forward with remembrances and anniversaries, writing still as I unpack it. I can't predict what I might write some spring morning when I see the first trillium unfold in Mary Young Park, or watch the delightful showering of rhododendron petals drop near the McLean House. Both our parents received bonus years, others finish this earthly life journey well before anyone might anticipate. Individual losses strike our hearts differently, making us into who we are today. Grief is raw and individual, no matter how we feel or express it. It is this raw emotion, whether shared in private or together, that unites us all.

The first time I paddled a kayak I borrowed a boat and floated Missoula's nearby Milltown Pond. Soon after I attempted to roll a kayak after spilling into a set of rapids on the Blackfoot River. Once underwater I pulled out and kicked my boat to the shore. While I am always cautious around water, I too have no great fears.

Ten years ago I bought my own boat. These days it is my solo ventures in quiet stretches of my home river that most fill my heart. I set out early in my quest to paddle tranquil favorite Willamette River stretches nearby. Glassy conditions trigger more of a rush in me than a double espresso. Today, in the season of fishing, I don't worry as I spy boat trailers at the landing just a few minutes from my house. I know they've gone upriver in search of fish near the mouth of the Clackamas or the Falls. I lean in and head downriver to explore still water.

I stop paddling and allow the slow, mindful current to engulf me. I let go. It's a metaphor for much in my life now. I am working to learn the art of letting go. This has not been my strongest suit this far. Determined I've been to make things happen, change things, get what I seek. And now: yes, it's time to let go. Bit by bit. It's not always easy.

During this last decade I've thought about how much my four siblings and I got from our parents; how differently we turned out. I had been thinking about how it happened that I received enough encouragement and support, without the helicopter demands and expectation to subject me to unfulfilled dreams of perfectionism.

Or, am I being honest with myself? I recognize the struggle I too sometimes have to figure out when enough is enough.

As I enter Oswego Creek from the Willamette I'm bombarded with a seasonal storm of cottonwood fibers. Those not from here might for an instant mistake it as an out of season snowstorm. I stop paddling. Branches sag laden with soggy leaves, the river level reaching higher than normal on its banks. White fibers encircle my boat and I drift in a soothing river scum. I paddle again, keenly aware of my solitude on the river. I lose myself in thoughts until I spot a stationary heron on the shore only feet away. I cease paddling to watch; the current turns my boat back downriver. I float, my eyes fixed on the bird until it gathers its wings and flies above the trees.

Maybe now in my Crone years, I too can embrace myself fully at this time of life. When Mom turned sixty, she held a crone party complete with a smudging ritual. As Mom's friends shared stories about aging, my toddler daughter hesitated before quietly explaining how her hands become wrinkled after her bath. I didn't throw a crone party when I turned sixty, but instead finalized a novel and grieved as Mom lay dying. A year later my spouse threw me a surprise party to acknowledge a difficult but important work transition I had made. And only on this most recent sixty-second birthday did I feel ready to throw that celebratory party welcoming me into this next stage.

I have been thinking about what I *now* know, need, and want, and those lessons passed on to me from my mom. Some say the Crone Stage of womanhood includes an ability to share wisdom. Are we better staged to reach into our deep spiritual self, to utilize our powers of intuition and find meaning? It is our time to give back, speak up, take action, and cultivate our passions. I have been slow to realize: I am among the last of my career peers still in a traditionally structured career. Yes, this is me. Now.

Maybe now I will better practice the art of letting go. Thank you, Mom. Through you I better understand my need to do this. We practice this throughout our life, with losses taxing our heart in ways we didn't before imagine. Letting go of anger, deception, and sometimes hopes, dreams, good health, and life itself. Perhaps, rather than letting go we recraft, repurpose, or redevelop.

Mom left us kids and grandkids with advice. I believe she would wish to share it with others if given the chance.

> My deepest hope and prayer is that my children and grandchildren learn from my history. That they will love and care for their bodies, stretch their minds, and grow spiritually as each day passes. That they wisely use their innate high energy levels and love themselves and others with passion, gratitude, and respect. That they live their lives with creativity and morality, and they, unlike my generation, make the world a better place for all living things. Even when I am gone physically, I will remain around, about and within each of them as a sense of deep, unending love.

And so, what am I to do now? Pursue still water and floating cotton fibers. Find joy in the simplest of things. The smile of a new baby. The opening of a pink wild rose. A sparkling midnight sky glittering with stars and planets. Join with friends and family. Write, teach, and speak out. And make time to seek more still water.

Elegies

Mourning in Pandemic Times

I miss her.

This mother of mine. My missing of her is different than that of Dad. He who already left this earth.

I'm an unknown shape to her through the window unless it's a good day. She sees the darkness in my hair. Outline of my lips in a smile against the paleness of my skin.

My wave a confusing blur to these eyes no longer seeing clearly. My voice garbled on a speaker.

I remind her. Your daughter. Your favorite. Only. You, my mother. My favorite. My only.

She smiles. Sometimes. On good days she laughs.

But if it is her daughter, why don't I come in and hug her? I remind her, and she nods her head. Slowly. In sad agreement.

I sing to her and on good days she sings along. I go slowly so she can keep up. A delay between my phone and what I barely hear as the speaker echoes through the window. I sing another. She shakes her head and says no. Is it too sentimental? Good times then, not now? Suddenly she is disturbed. Songs like that don't belong in this weird world that none of us can understand including her.

I read to her, selecting only funny or simple stories through this complicated communication. On good days she laughs, smiles, nods along. On bad days she closes her eyes. Asleep or elsewhere, I'm not sure.

My voice catches. No crying. I can't cry, not now. I need to be the strong one. I need to pretend: yes, all is well. Stop the tears now. Until later. After.

All I want to do is sit outside in the sun and hold her hand.

No words. Stare at the blue of the sky and the green of the firs. Peer out into this magical world, blurry for her, clear for me.

Nature that is strangely still here. Wondrous and awakening in the spring with peachy tulips rimmed with yellow, laden catkins drooping from maples.

Yes, I say. We are lucky. Some of the lucky ones. I don't feel lucky.

She has had a good life. A long one. She knows. But not now. Not as she had hoped it would be now.

Me too: family, children, a paying job and benefits, roof over my head and food in the pantry. And yet I cry. More tears stream today than yesterday in this passage of time. After each window visit and telephone call and facetime.

Many more days than not I now hope she might pass peacefully one night. Soon.

But not soon if we can't see her?

Not too soon for her to laugh at grandsons and smile with her only daughter and granddaughters and sons with faces close enough to know. To smell and feel our love.

Not too soon to be out in the green and blue together again.

And yet. We're lucky. We are the fortunate ones. Tears drip. I grieve.

I miss her.

This mother of mine.

Where Do Memories Go?

Where do memories go when they leave you? When the *you* I know, no longer is the *you* I see. Are souvenirs of life's moments sucked up by vacuum in one fell swoop, to be sprinkled back to where they came from? Or do they float away, disappearing image by image, until it is as if they never were? Recycling back into a universe we love and fear, and mostly don't understand.

The remembrance of the first glimpse of morning sun to strike a tent, peeking out between summer washed peaks. You, crawling, barefooted to scramble out into the newly forming day, birds replacing alarm clocks, evening mosquitoes already dissipated in the gathered warmth of the day. Your knowledge: only *this* moment matters. Only *this* moment is real. A moment shared with no one.

Now. That and other memories hidden. Sucked away as if they never happened. Mostly. Except that one time—oh, pray that it comes again—when something jars it loose, spilling a recollection forth in a confusing array of *almost goodness* coupled with confusion. Where did it come from? Crumbs seeping back into an almost awareness of sensing cool air and anticipation of something else. Quick! Grab it before it disappears. Hold it dear. Bless it. Know that it may not come again.

Like the glistening, wet snowflakes, that once solicited you from a warm bed, to dash out on a morning dance in gray and white on a Willamette Valley winter day. To get there before they melt as if never existing to begin with. The wet flakes now land on a toddler's lashes as she grasps the gloved hand of a different grandmother: one who can still see and hear. One who both makes and still holds memories.

Life is for the moment. We who are lucky, in *who* those moments return. Until they don't. We who are not lucky, but fortunate to have others to bring those moments back to us. Patiently, we hope. Until they no longer do. When they are no longer our memories, but those circling the universe. Memories of someone else who we may have known. Or a character in a story. Or a mother, daughter, father or son. Memories *are* for yesterday. The bad we seem eager to have yanked from us. The good we plead to stay. To come again and comfort us among our moments of today. Yet, life *is* for the moment. Where do memories go when they leave us?

Sadness in the Beauty of the Day

Sadness in the beauty of the day.

My cold fingers ache in half finger cycling gloves, yet early morning sun shines bright enough to need shades.

I feel sad in the beauty of it.

Sad for those I miss who no longer are here.

Sad for those who no longer are as they once were.

The stillness of the air, and ripples of the river brings it out, from within.

This Willamette stretch I know so well.

Yet.
Suddenly five crows caw.
Dart with each other in a circular chase.
Louder, louder, louder, as if to still my brain.
Quiet my own circular musings.
I am not human-centric enough to believe I know why they do
what they do.
Or what they do, when they do it.
Yet, it stills me and slows my pedaling feet.
As if to say:
Stop.
Leave it.
The day is beautiful.
Rejoice.
It is all that we have.
Rejoice.
Beauty in the sadness.
Sadness in the beauty of the day.

Acknowledgements

I'm grateful for my publisher, Bedazzled Ink Publishing, who has supported my creativity and desire to share my heart.

This work would not be what it is without the bimonthly support of my virtual writing group. Thank you Leigh, Maura, Michael, Emily and Shelly. Few spaces exist that feel as safe as ours.

I thank Patty's dearest friends, sisters, nieces, nephews and brother-in-laws, students and colleagues for encouragement, sharing memories and supporting me on this work.

Above all, I thank our mom, Patty Marilyn Daum Montgomery, for being who she was. I honor her persevering, touching so many people in her life and finding it important to record her thoughts, experiences and life lessons. I'm grateful for the miracle that mixed passion, chromosomes and grit so to allow me to be raised by this amazing woman. I honor my husband Russ, our daughters, my brothers and families, and our dad for supporting our experience of being part of this woman's life until her last breath. And beyond.

Dede Montgomery is the author of *My Music Man, Beyond the Ripples, Then, Now and In-Between: Place, Memories and Loss in Oregon*, and *Humanity's Grace*. Dede is a 6th generation Oregonian and lives near Portland, Oregon.

Learn more at https://dedemontgomery.com

Aim your phone's camera at the QR Code.

9 781960 373403